Customer-Centric Project Management

Customer-Centric Project Management

ELIZABETH HARRIN

and

PHIL PEPLOW

Routledge
Taylor & Francis Group

LONDON AND NEW YORK

First published 2012 by Ashgate Publishing

Published 2016 by Routledge
2 Park Square, Milton Park, Abingdon, Oxon OX14 4RN
711 Third Avenue, New York, NY 10017, USA

Routledge is an imprint of the Taylor & Francis Group, an informa business

British Library Cataloguing in Publication Data
Harrin, Elizabeth.
  Customer-centric project management. -- (Advances in
  project management)
  1. Project management. 2. Customer relations.
  I. Title II. Series III. Peplow, Phil.
  658.4'04-dc23

  ISBN 9781409443124 (pbk)

Library of Congress Cataloging-in-Publication Data
Harrin, Elizabeth.
  Customer-centric project management / by Elizabeth Harrin and Phil Peplow.
    p. cm. -- (Advances in project management)
  Includes bibliographical references and index.
  ISBN 978-1-4094-4312-4 (pbk)
  1. Project management. 2. Customer relations. I. Peplow, Phil.
  II. Title.
  HD69.P75H359 2012
  658.4'04--dc23

                                                              2012018935

CONTENTS

LIST OF FIGURES

LIST OF TABLES

ACKNOWLEDGEMENTS

Customer-centric project management is about engaging with others, and we have done that in the production of this book. We would like to thank the managers who let us test these ideas at their companies, the people who have routinely responded to Exceed meetings so positively and the project managers and project teams who have also engaged in the spirit of Exceed in an effort to improve the way in which projects are delivered. Without support for the concept of customer-centric project management, it would have remained an academic idea. Instead, we have been able to test it and see the results.

We'd also like to thank Jonathan Norman at Gower and Darren Dalcher at the National Centre for Project Management at Middlesex University.

ABOUT THE AUTHORS

ELIZABETH HARRIN

Elizabeth Harrin MA, MBCS, FAPM, is a project and programme manager with over a decade of experience managing information technology (IT) and business change projects. Her experience spans the financial services and healthcare industries and she has a wide breadth of knowledge in project management topics including the uses of social media in a project environment.

Elizabeth has spoken at numerous conferences in Europe and the United States. She is the author of *Project Management in the Real World* (BCS Books, 2006) and *Social Media for Project Managers* (PMI, 2010). She also writes and publishes the award-winning blog, A Girl's Guide to Project Management (www. GirlsGuideToPM.com), and was named IT Professional Blogger of the Year by *Computer Weekly* in 2011.

Elizabeth also runs The Otobos Group, a project management communications consultancy. Educated at the University of York and Roehampton University, Elizabeth is a Fellow of the Association for Project Management, a PRINCE2, MSP and P3O Practitioner and a member of the Project Management Institute.

PHIL PEPLOW

Phil Peplow is an IT service delivery director with more than 30 years' experience in the management of service organizations. His industry experience includes manufacturing, retail, financial services, investment banking, travel, networking, healthcare and IT outsourcing.

Phil has led global IT organizations with operations across EMEA, North America, Australia and India. He has also worked as a consultant and operations director for two global investment banks in the City of London.

Phil's project experience includes the rollout of a number of global IT process improvement and delivery initiatives. An ITIL certified professional, Phil is also a student of the INSEAD graduate business school at Fontainebleau.

Phil's speciality is creating best-in-class IT organizations which deliver exceptionally high levels of customer satisfaction.

PRAISE FOR EXCEED AND CUSTOMER-CENTRIC PROJECT MANAGEMENT

'The Exceed process is incredibly powerful. It allows the IT service function to be measured in the only way that matters – by the customer – while at the same time providing guidance on how to improve things. The process is also incredibly straightforward, so it provides a basis for really meaningful dialogue with your customers.'

Marc O'Brien, former CIO, Spire Healthcare

'I utilize the Exceed document from Spire Healthcare to educate and continually improve the Agfa Service desk, remote and field personnel alike. It is a very useful tool to directly measure end user satisfaction whilst plotting discernible improvement and feeding back to my teams and upper Agfa management.'

Rob Harwood, Service Delivery Manager, Agfa Healthcare

'Exceed allowed us to achieve fantastic results in terms of customer satisfaction. It enabled us to channel our energies into precisely what our customers were looking for – a consistently excellent service.'

Neil Harrison, CEO, Travelex

INTRODUCTION

Let's get some basics established. Projects must deliver value. Projects must involve stakeholders, even if that stakeholder population is made up of only one person. These two things are the premise for this book. The third premise is that stakeholders are the ones who get to decide what 'value' actually means.

The traditional approach to project management is that successful project delivery is predicated on managing by the triple constraint of time, cost and quality. Project managers assess a project as successful if it delivers on time, within budget and to the required quality criteria set for project scope. However, times are changing. Project management academics and practitioners are moving towards defining project success as the delivery of organizational value in the form of business results.

The increased interest and take up in project, programme and portfolio offices (P3Os) demonstrates this. James Pennypacker (2009) writes that project portfolio management 'at its best … is concerned with the role of top management and key decision-makers in creating purposeful project investments and in formulating and implementing goals and objectives'. Deloitte Consulting has developed a Results Management Office model that changes the focus of the traditional Programme Management Office (PMO) into one that includes a distinct bias towards delivering business value and embedded organizational change, regardless of whether the original time, cost and quality metrics are met.[1]

The value discussion in the literature has taken two distinct directions. There is the discussion of the value of project management as a discipline (see, for example, Thomas and Mullaly 2008, and Zhai et al. 2009) and the discussion around calculating the organizational value of project deliverables, in other words, whether projects achieve gains for organizational strategy or corporate objectives. Despite all these conversations about value, there still remains a disconnect between the

---

1   For more on RMOs, see http://www.deloitte.com/view/en_US/us/Services/consulting/ technology-consulting/12f2be8ed4847210VgnVCM100000ba42f00aRCRD.htm [accessed: 22 April 2012]

way projects are managed and the people they are being delivered for. And no one can really agree on what 'value' is.

Project management traditionally talks about stakeholders: people who have a stake in the outcome of the project. Sometimes, the term 'stakeholder' is used as a euphemism for 'most important or senior person' or 'individual who is paying for the project'. The people whom project teams care most about are defined by the deliverables that are created for them, not the way in which they are delivered.

We believe that it's time to rethink value, and rethink stakeholder management. Those people are not only stakeholders; they are customers of the project management process, and they get to decide what's valuable. Project teams deliver a service, and should provide excellent customer service along with the deliverables that the project is producing. Project customers can be individuals or teams at all levels, colleagues or third-party providers, and they should all get similar treatment. The person who holds the purse strings is not the only one who gets to decide if the project team is doing a good job. These days, everyone matters – more than they ever have before. Working together is the only (and best) way to deliver projects successfully.

The disconnect between the 'stakeholder' approach and the 'customer' approach is evident in the fact that traditional project management methods only ask stakeholders for their feedback on the project process at the post-implementation review. In restaurants, good customer service generally means interrupting your conversation with fellow diners to ask if your meal is OK. As annoying as this can be, restaurants have created the opportunity to check customer satisfaction at several points throughout their interaction with the customer. The post-implementation review process is the opposite of this: the equivalent of a waiter leaving drinks, all three courses and a pot of coffee on the table and then disappearing until the end of the night when he materializes with the bill.

Of course, project management isn't quite like that. Stakeholders are involved in the elicitation of requirements and should be involved in testing. In fact, there are numerous ways to involve stakeholders during the life of a project. But project teams don't tend to ask them how they are feeling about the project management processes, or assess the project management processes themselves until the project is over.

How are you feeling? Project managers don't like having that type of conversation. They focus on the capture of lessons learned: an inwardly focused step with the lessons ploughed back into the evolution of processes for the next project. Even Agile projects that heavily involve the user don't typically ask them what they feel about the project.

We know this is changing. In fact, we know project managers who love talking to project customers about how they feel things are going. It's an opportunity to find out what is working and what is troubling the customer. It's a chance to put things right before they go too wrong. And customers love having someone listen.

This is a book about customer-centric project management. It's about why customers matter more than post-implementation reviews, and what to do when you realize that customers are the most important thing about the project – any project. You might have heard a lot of talk about 'engagement' but not really worked out how to do it. This book will show you how. In Chapter 1 we introduce Exceed, which is a tool (a simple spreadsheet) and a process (also very easy) to 'do' engagement with project customers.

In Chapter 2 we discuss why customers are your most important project stakeholder, and why you should engage with them comprehensively to give yourself the best possible chance of project success.

We recognize that there is a shift towards better engagement with stakeholders, and Chapter 3 looks at this. We call this way of working 'collaborative project management', which is where the success of the project hinges on a team working well together. We argue that we need to go further than collaboration to get to true customer centricity.

Chapter 4 discusses how project performance and success is currently measured by PMOs and stakeholders. We also talk about the limitations of post-implementation reviews, but if you are hoping that by reading this book you'll never have to do another post-implementation review again, you'd be wrong. Recording what went well and what didn't is still a good thing, and the methods for capturing lessons learned have evolved and improved over the years. The Cabinet Office's P3O standard, for example, has a project maturity model that requires continuous process improvement and organizational capture of lessons learned in order to achieve Level 4 maturity.

Chapters 5 and 6 discuss our own experiences at being customer-centric. As you'll see from our case study, customers don't define success as the traditional triple constraint view of time, cost and quality. Project managers could deliver on time, on budget and exceeding quality measures every time but still be considered ineffective by their internal or external customers.

Today, business environments are more complex than ever before. Stakeholders want project managers to use approaches that help the business succeed. Chapter 7 looks at how to refine your customer-centric approach to take the needs of stakeholders into account.

If we are genuinely going to deliver value through projects we continually need to discuss what 'value' means with our stakeholders. Chapter 8 provides a straightforward implementation guide to moving your own business to a customer-centric way of working, using the Exceed process.

Finally, in Chapter 9 we provide some guidance about ensuring that customer centricity is sustainable and supported in the organization.

This is a short book, but – we think – a big idea. *Customer-Centric Project Management* will show you why collaborative project management is good, but why customer-centric project management is better. And you'll find out how to implement Exceed in your own organization so that you can benefit from increased customer-satisfaction levels in your stakeholder community.

Customer satisfaction does get mentioned in some of the project management literature around post-implementation reviews. In their book on value-driven project management, Kerzner and Saladis (2009: 233) write: 'The last life-cycle phase is customer-satisfaction management. This is the phase where BPs (best practices) and lessons learned are captured.' This post-implementation review phase is the way project managers and project processes improve within organizations. Unfortunately, even when customer satisfaction is considered, it still comes at the end of a project. By that point, it's too late to send your starter back if it is cold (to carry on our restaurant analogy) and there is no opportunity to order another bottle of wine. Leaving the discussion about process and satisfaction until the end of the project does not enable stakeholders to benefit from the lessons that have been captured. The end of the project is far too late to change the project management approach in order to better meet the customers' requirements.

Stakeholders are happy to talk about what they value and how they feel, if we ask them in a timely manner and are prepared to listen to and act on what they say. You can listen to customers more effectively, and this book explains how. We wrote *Customer-Centric Project Management* to help project managers understand how to engage stakeholders in discussions about project value and success, without having to wait until the end of the project to do so. This book takes post-implementation reviews and lessons learned approaches to the next level.

If you want to continuously engage stakeholders, the post-implementation review process is not adequate, so you need an alternative process to support and record those discussions. The Exceed process for customer-satisfaction scoring was developed by Phil Peplow while he was leading a number of IT service delivery organizations, the function tasked with delivering the day-to-day technology services that keep businesses going. In 2010, the Exceed process was adapted for use with project teams and project customers. 'Project Exceed' has been in use at Spire Healthcare since then, and this has had a direct impact on improving customer satisfaction within the IT services and project management practices at the company. The immediacy and simplicity of the feedback mechanism enables project teams to identify dissatisfaction in the project management process early and thus resolve it. Putting the customer at the heart of how we do projects and using the Exceed process to tangibly record levels of engagement, means that we can improve the chances of project success through continual and specifically relevant stakeholder dialogue.

Being customer-centric is a journey. Project managers don't suddenly change their entire outlook overnight, and talking about the customers is different from actually listening to them and acting in their best interests. Using tools and processes to guide customer-centric thinking helps project managers see the results of engagement and demonstrate how things can improve, even on difficult projects.

Unlike many books presenting the results of empirical study, our case study did not start with the academic desire to prove a hypothesis. We are customer-centric because it's the right thing to be. We use the Exceed process in our workplace because it's practical to do so. We wanted to improve how we managed projects, and experience showed us that we could. Elizabeth Harrin had already started reading and researching the academic background to value management in a project environment, and together we realized that there was a big chunk missing – the chunk about customer satisfaction and a practical model to manage and measure it.

In this book we use the terms 'project customer' and 'stakeholder' interchangeably. It's easier, and we hope it contributes to a debate about levels of customer service provided to project stakeholders. Regardless of what we call the people who have an interest in the project, the approach of waiting until the end does not fit with the way in which work is carried out today and the way in which stakeholders (customers) wish to be involved in projects.

WHO SHOULD READ THIS BOOK?

This book is for anyone who wants to move on from post-implementation reviews and really understand what project stakeholders want. It's relevant for:

- intermediate- and advanced-level project managers in both the public and private sectors;
- programme managers looking to ensure continuous stakeholder engagement and satisfaction for the duration of a programme;
- portfolio managers looking to cement the value proposition of a portfolio: statistical assessment of project customers' perception will help prove the case for the P3O;

- academics researching stakeholder value or project management value. The case study in the book is a starting point for future research.

Given that the roots of our customer-centric thinking are in the IT industry, this book draws heavily on the authors' IT backgrounds and technology projects as examples. However, we believe that the concepts of customer-centric project management are applicable to all project environments, so readers from all industries will be able to use these concepts to better understand the needs of their stakeholders.

Knowing what you want to do and how to go about it is not the same as success. We can't guarantee that the Exceed process will radically improve project success rates, and no process can. Adopting a customer-centric mindset and using the Exceed process to measure and monitor customer satisfaction will, however, help you move towards working with happier, more engaged stakeholders. That was our goal for this book: to carry on the discussion of value and to help project teams deliver more successfully through better engagement with stakeholders. However, you will not see any benefit yourself from just reading *Customer-Centric Project Management*. Results come from action, so read on, and then take some concrete steps to identifying, working with and talking to your project customers.

CHAPTER 1

INTRODUCING A CUSTOMER-CENTRIC PROCESS

A lot has been written about stakeholder management and the importance of communication (more on that later), but there are few practical models relating to how to engage people in projects. If you want to work in a customer-centric way, you need to arm yourself with tools to help you do so. Exceed is a practical model to use as the basis for stakeholder communications. It is a proven process designed to deliver services which consistently and continually deliver exceptional levels of customer satisfaction. In short, while customer-centric project management is a state of mind, Exceed is the practical manifestation that shows you how customer-centric you really are. It's the process of defining how well a business, department or team is perceived by its customers.

Knowing how good customers think you are is not the same as being customer-centric. Only by acting on their feedback will you get to high levels of service and customer satisfaction. There are eight steps in the Exceed process which allow you to act on the output from the feedback that customers provide. Exceed, when implemented professionally, will also ensure that high levels of satisfaction are maintained throughout the life of a project.

Putting customers – and by that we mean internal colleagues or third-party partners who take a service from another department – at the heart of how we work is a worthy aim. Companies spend a lot of time on focus groups and surveying end customers – consumers who buy products – but not a lot of time looking at how departments within the company serve each other. There might be an annual staff satisfaction survey which is the opportunity to air views on how different teams work together, but this type of conversation is rarely routine. Once you realize that as a team you have internal customers too, making yourself easy to do business with is the next logical step. Customer centricity is a mindset, a way of working. It is, however, very hard to measure attitudes and behaviours in any unequivocal way.

Exceed was designed to provide an unequivocal way to answer the key question that keeps senior executives in PMOs and other delivery teams awake at night: how good is my organization? To answer that, you need clarity of customer perception, a focus on customer engagement and the deliverables that matter to project customers. The process is based on uncovering the top issues and asking customers to score project teams against a number of variables. This allows committed businesses or functions to move beyond the rhetoric and to demonstrate unequivocally how good their service or project performance really is on a day-to-day basis.

THE ORIGINS OF EXCEED

The customer-centric process was developed to establish the basis of real agreement about the value being provided to stakeholders, and to develop closer engagement with customers using language that everyone could relate to. A global financial services company successfully implemented a customer-centric approach in its IT department. The IT service delivery function was already highly efficient, having demonstrated continual successes through a number of initiatives. Rationalization, in-sourcing and outsourcing had delivered operational savings of over £1m for three consecutive years. A further project to implement a technical support centre with a 50-strong team in India within nine months of board approval reduced annual spend by a further £1.8m. This project was completed without disruption to service, on time and to budget and proved the ability of IT to successfully deliver complex technical and sensitive projects in a very short timescale.

Shortly after this latest success, the chief information officer found himself in a frustrating position. The head of the company's retail division had rung him to complain that the software updates his team desperately needed had not been implemented as promised.

The CIO's department had a record of regular cost reduction and project delivery. That very week, the retail division had benefited from a further £250,000 cost reduction, delivered directly to this manager's bottom line as a result of a telecoms contract renegotiation carried out by IT. However, without the software updates, retail branches could not satisfy their customers. The financial results may have been good, but they did nothing to improve customer service or the perception of IT within the retail division.

There are a number of morals to this story. Delivery organizations – and project teams are delivery organizations – need to clearly understand how to fully satisfy *all* of their customers' needs *at all* times and in every situation. There also needs to be an agreed and credible process which proves the quality of the level of service being provided. In this case the IT team was doing a good job. Or were they? Who thought so? In fact, what really defines success for an organization, project or service and how do we measure and quantify it? After all, customers and stakeholders come in all shapes and sizes. They are not only demanding – their requirements are diverse and not always feasible or realistic.

Customer-centric thinking cuts through the confusion by answering a number of key questions:

- How professional is my operation?
- How good are we at delivering services or projects?
- What does good look like for us?

These are the questions that need answering if you are going to truly be customer-centric. Exceed is the process we use to get there.

It begins with a vision: *'Every customer of company/department/project team XYZ will continually rate the services we provide as Good, Very Good or Excellent.'*

That's one sentence. The economy of language is deliberate: every word is important in articulating the essence of good customer service. Let's look at those words again:

- *Every customer of*: all customers of company/department/project team XYZ must be represented through a collaborative partnership with the project team.
- *will continually rate*: regular and continual customer dialogue is key to being customer-centric.
- *the services we provide*: there must be a clear focus on the deliverables from company/department/project team XYZ.
- *as Good, Very Good or Excellent*: customers measure the perceived value they receive in a simple, deliberately subjective way. This is the heart of being customer-centric. It is what the customer thinks is important that counts.

If you haven't worked it out yet, the single overriding principle behind the Exceed process is customer satisfaction. We believe that this is the only credible and worthwhile measure of an organization's success. Customer-centric project management puts customer satisfaction at the heart of project management with the aim of ensuring all project customers believe the project team is delivering a quality service. Exceed shows whether you are achieving that or not.

This is a shift from standard quality measurements which are usually internal and 'rear view' in nature. In a PMO, earned value management metrics, number of submitted scope changes, cumulative project slip, effort overruns, overtime worked and quality control statistics (all diagnostic project metrics discussed in Kendrick 2012) are hardly likely to energize customers. These metrics tend to relate almost entirely to issues which had a negative effect on their lives and are almost always yesterday's news.

Measurement of service quality in both project and operational environments is often limited to the performance of processes that the customer has a right to expect as standard. No project sponsor begins the project expecting that the measures of time, cost and quality will be ignored (the classic triple constraint of project management) or that tolerance levels will be exceeded. There is the understanding that change could create a situation where time, cost and quality would need to be revisited, but by hiring a competent project manager there is the expectation that these measures will be achieved. This is the hygiene factor for projects; the basic levels of service that project customers expect as standard from their project teams. We should not expect to get credit for what our internal customers take for granted.[1] Failing to fully engage with project customers means that what they actually consider important can be overlooked while we pat ourselves on the back for doing what they hired us for in the first place.

Even with a fledgling appreciation of the role of customer satisfaction in project management, project teams can struggle to convince their customers of the wonderful service they receive. They rarely, if ever, gather metrics to justify the value of project management (Thomas and Mullaly 2008). Part of the reason for this is that projects are a journey and our existing metrics are not. Time, cost and quality measures do not adequately reflect the nature of the experience along the way. You can travel 10 miles in a Rolls Royce Corniche or walk along the roadside barefoot and reach your destination in an acceptable time but the experience of both journeys is quite different. Customer-centric approaches like Exceed provide an opportunity to work collaboratively with customers to elicit success criteria, define new metrics and track them in a meaningful way throughout the entire project journey.

Remember our fed-up CIO from the beginning of this chapter? The Exceed process in his department began with the simple vision that we saw earlier: *'Every customer of IT service delivery will continually rate the services we provide as Good, Very Good or Excellent'*. Experienced (or dare we say cynical?) managers would be forgiven for thinking that this vision could never be achieved. However, the team achieved rapid results from the first few weeks and they fully achieved this vision in less than six months.

---

1   One of the senior executives we have worked with – who shall remain nameless – summed this up by saying, 'No one applauds when you flush the toilet.' In other words, there are some things that people simply expect to work and that you should never expect to get any credit for.

There wasn't anything special about this particular CIO or his organization. It was just about putting the customer front and centre and working in a customer-centric way. As a process, Exceed has worked in a number of companies and industries. The Exceed process was initially created for use in IT but has been used successfully within financial services, logistics and healthcare businesses. The case study starting in Chapter 5 discusses the implementation of Exceed in another company in a different industry. Before we get there, though, let's take a step back and look at why what customers think is increasingly important in today's business environment.

KEY POINTS:

- Customers are people who receive a service from another department or third-party partner. They are customers of the project management process.
- Customer-centric project management puts customer satisfaction at the heart of project management with the aim of ensuring all project customers believe the project team is delivering a quality service.
- Exceed is a proven process which shows whether you are achieving that or not. It's designed to help teams deliver services which consistently and continually deliver exceptional levels of customer satisfaction.
- Exceed is expressed as a vision: 'Every customer of this department will continually rate the services we provide as Good, Very Good or Excellent.'
- Exceed provides an opportunity to work collaboratively with customers to elicit success criteria and track them in a meaningful way throughout the entire project journey.

CHAPTER 2

WHY CUSTOMERS COUNT

'Projects are investments undertaken to create value (economic or social in non-profit environments) for the project's stakeholders,' write Thomas G. Lechler and John C. Byrne in their book, *The Mindset for Creating Project Value* (2010). If we take this as the reason why projects are done in the first place, generating value from project activity is essential.

Project management methods do not guarantee value. They guarantee (or go some way to offering a guarantee, if you want to hedge your bets) that projects will deliver according to the agreed corporate standards and within defined tolerances. In fact, implementing project management processes does not guarantee a return on investment from those processes, and research shows that even where tangible benefits from a project management implementation are being delivered, they are not quantified (Thomas and Mullaly 2008).

So while on the one hand we use project management processes that don't guarantee value, on the other we are still measuring value through the triple constraint. 'The goal of getting "projects done right" is to have projects come in on time, on budget, and meeting all quality standards,' write Weinstein and Jaques (2009: 354) – and that is their prediction for how things will be in 2025. There is something missing from this definition of 'done right': the people who receive the output of the project and who want to do something useful with it.

As any project manager will know, projects do not exist in a vacuum. They are created from the need to fulfil an organizational objective such as generating more revenue or improving brand awareness. Projects happen because someone – an individual or a committee – deems that this particular initiative will deliver some kind of business benefit. Typically, the person who stands to gain the most value from a project becomes the project sponsor. For example, the sales director would sponsor a project to install new customer management software, providing the sales team with more opportunities to cross-sell to the existing customer base. The sponsor receives the output from the project and wants to do something with it to achieve those organizational objectives.

Creating a successful project team involves ensuring excellent links between the 'permanent' project employees – those who work predominantly in a projectized way such as project managers and business analysts – and those who have joined a project team on a secondment basis as a subject matter expert or stakeholder. Project teams are made up of wide groups of diverse professionals, and ensuring that stakeholders are engaged in the project process is essential to the success of the project. Close working relationships with the project customer are important.

Project management and business change have been two sides of the same coin for some time. Project management delivers a specific product, and business change ensures that this product is effectively used and embedded in the organization. However, the lines between these two disciplines are – and should be – blurring.

Today it is no longer adequate for project management teams to work in isolation on their projects, focusing solely on delivering a product and ignoring the context in which it is to be used. Part of understanding the project's context is for project managers to understand the rationale behind their project, the business context and the business change required in order for the company to achieve value from the project deliverables. To put it another way, if you don't know why you are working on a project you shouldn't be working on it at all. Resources are too scarce to invest time in projects that do not contribute to strategic or operational objectives.

WHO IS THE PROJECT CUSTOMER?

In this book, we use the terms 'customer', 'project customer' and 'stakeholder' interchangeably (and we use 'consumer' for the end user who buys or uses a product once a project has completed). Traditionally, stakeholders could include both individuals and groups like government agencies, regulatory bodies or 'the public'. While the project manager may have kept these groups in mind during the project, they were perhaps represented by a focus group, an individual or not represented actively on the project at all.

Project customers are those stakeholders with a significant vested interest in the outcome of the project. This includes the project sponsor and any other executive providing resources for the project. It could also include those who will be the customer of the end product, for example, the Senior User in PRINCE2 terminology.

In many respects, it doesn't really matter how you define customer, or how many customers your project has. What is important is that by shifting the terminology of the project team from 'stakeholder' to 'customer' the team starts thinking about the people involved as individuals who require a service from the project management team, as well as a deliverable at the end of the project. That is the mindset change for customer-centric project management.

BEING CUSTOMER-CENTRIC

The shift we believe is essential for the long-term success of project management as a profession is to move away from a deliverable focus ('I've done what you asked') and towards a value-driven focus ('I've delivered something you should find beneficial').

This attitude change makes project managers more aware of how what they do delivers value for the project's internal or external customer. It goes further than the Cabinet Office's approach to benefit management embedded in the Managing Successful Programmes framework; projects that are not aligned to a programme have no inherent way of ensuring that value is generated, as the prevalent methodologies are deliverable-focused.

Once you have decided that you want to shift to a better working relationship with project customers, you need a way to measure and monitor how you are doing. Exceed, as we saw in the previous chapter, is a process designed to do just that by capturing value criteria and giving the project management team the appropriate opportunities to explore and record progress against these.

Capturing value criteria is essential, and these should be directly related to what the customer feels is important. The value a project delivers is usually a consequence of the rationale for doing the project in the first place (Kendrick 2012), but 'value' means different things to different people so each of your customers will have a different interpretation of why and how they will get value from working with a project manager on this initiative.

Customer-centric project management captures these value criteria and aligns the goals of the project and the services of the project manager with the requirements and needs of the most important people on the project: the customers. Projects are done by people, for other people, and maintaining a two-way dialogue is essential to ensure that what is delivered is fit for purpose and meets the customers' expectations, especially as value is a property that emerges over time and is context-dependent. In other words, the expectations of your customers may change (Preble 2005) during the life of the project as they discover more about the project deliverables, the proposed benefits and the organizational environment in which they will be used, but they still dictate the value proposition.

Taking a customer-centric approach to project management requires maintaining dialogue and understanding what is important to project stakeholders. They cannot be seen as a low-level annoyance factor, a group of people who submit change requests and make 'unreasonable' demands. Partnering with project customers should minimize the changes that the project manager considers unexpected and make the working relationship better.

Essential to partnering is dialogue. You can only know what is important to stakeholders if you take the time to ask them. A Norwegian study shows that customer satisfaction in a project environment is growing in importance: it wasn't on the radar in 2000 but when researchers compared what was important on projects in 2008, satisfied customers suddenly appeared as one of the key criteria (Andersen 2010). Several studies show that project management practices can affect customer satisfaction (see for example Papke-Shields et al. 2010, Andersen 2010), so the project manager is in a great position to be able to directly influence satisfaction levels and the outcome of the project through dialogue and collaborative working.

CUSTOMERS COUNT FOR PROJECT MANAGERS

Customer recommendations and testimonials are now commonplace in all professions and project management is no different. A project manager is only as good as his or her last project. A great reference or a glowing recommendation on LinkedIn can be a huge help when you apply for your next job. This type of meaningful referral – in contrast to a template reference from the corporate human resources function – typically comes from the project sponsor, who will most likely be the main project customer. Keeping customers happy can be an excellent career move, even when looking for internal promotions or to be given larger and more complex assignments in your current role.

Another personal benefit to engaging project customers fully is that constant dialogue builds credibility, trust and understanding on both sides and can help to make working relationships more effective and less stressful. A team that is motivated and focused on well-being has a greater chance of delivering projects successfully (Suhonen and Paasivaara 2011).

Sometimes customers are wary and fearful of change. They engage with the project under sufferance. Working in a customer-centric way can make the change less scary for project customers and improve motivation to participate in projects. Continual dialogue and a set of behaviours around providing a useful, meaningful service will help them feel more engaged. A process of continual dialogue helps wary customers engage in a non-threatening way.

A further benefit of this is that customers who feel as if they are genuinely part of the team are easier to work with, and less likely to be involved in disruptive conflict situations. Stress levels on projects can be substantial, especially when the project manager is dealing with major issues. Good customer relationships are one way to reduce stress levels: customers are more forgiving when a good relationship has been forged with them over time, as we will see from the case study in Chapter 6.

Unfortunately, many project managers are still assessed against their ability to deliver projects on time, on budget and to the required scope and quality. Their objectives are set rigidly to reflect the triple constraint. The downside of this is that they are actively incentivized to deliver against these criteria, and research by Papke-Shields et al. (2010) shows that the formal project management practices linked to the triple constraint are still the techniques most widely used. Salary increases, bonuses and other forms of employee recognition depend on delivering successfully against the targets set by line managers and organizations. If these do not reflect stakeholder satisfaction, stakeholder satisfaction will not be prioritized by the employee. The research by Papke-Shields et al. (2010) also shows that techniques related to communication are amongst those least used by project managers, which reflects the low priority that many organizations place on stakeholder engagement.

Part of making the move towards customer-centric project management is empowering line managers to set objectives for individuals and teams which include stakeholder satisfaction measures, so that the work environment is completely aligned to a model that delivers value and satisfaction instead of being hampered by the triple constraint.

CUSTOMERS COUNT FOR OPERATIONAL TEAMS

Projects are not (or should not be) done in isolation. When the project team has created the deliverable, installed the software or built the product, they move on to work on the next project, and an operational team will pick up the management of both the deliverable and the customer. In an IT software project, this would be the IT service delivery team who will take ongoing, day-to-day responsibility for the support and maintenance of the new software asset, including the relationship with the customers who use it. In a construction project, the building will be handed over to the new facilities management team, who will be responsible for its upkeep and maintenance and the relationship with the occupants and freeholder.

At project completion, project customers become business-as-usual customers, and a good relationship during the project stages of any initiative will set the stage for a good relationship with the operational team. Project managers can make the lives of their colleagues easier in the future by facilitating good working relationships with project customers now.

CUSTOMERS CARE ABOUT THE PROJECT NOW

Customer service happens at a given point in time, not four months into the future when a deliverable is complete. By changing the language we use to describe project stakeholders, we can also change our attitudes towards the service we provide for them. As you will know if you have ever waited a very long time for your order to be taken in a restaurant, or had to return an item to a shop, customers care about their experiences right now.

Customer-centric project management means taking account of how customers feel about a project at a given moment and then regularly reviewing that. The 'now' is the most important moment for value-driven projects. Customers care most about how projects are going now and the immediate impact this has on them, their colleagues and their business objectives. Of course 'now' as a moment in time changes from hour to hour which is why the Exceed process relies on regular dialogue between the project management team and the project customers. In every 'now' moment, project teams can ask themselves, 'Is the project perceived to be delivering value right now, and if not, what can I do to change that?'

Some customers may well have the long view and be appreciative of their project in the wider business context over a period of time. However, in our experience these are rare, and project stakeholders – while they all know the end goals and can see the longer-term plan – are far more concerned with today's problem of staffing levels or drop in revenue.

WHEN THE CUSTOMER ISN'T ALWAYS RIGHT

Customer-centric project management means making sure that the project is consistently able to meet the customers' expectations both in terms of deliverables and delivery methodology. However, what happens when the customer wants something that is not achievable? For example, in one of your regular conversations with the project sponsor, you receive the feedback that the change management process is unwieldy. Couldn't you simply be more flexible and incorporate changes as and when they come up?

An effective approach to project management requires a mature and robust change methodology, so the answer to this request would be no – a change management process is required. The project manager in this situation should also explain why this is the case. However, there may be some things you can do to reduce the bureaucracy of process for the customer, such as shortening the change request form, providing support on how to complete it, completing it for the customer or reducing the length of time the change approval process takes. Without this kind of feedback, you will be unable to find a way to really tailor the project experience for the customer, and potentially make it better for everyone, now and in the future.

Customer centricity does not require project managers to concede to every request. Project management processes and standards exist for a reason: years of best practices and lessons learned distilled into a project management methodology should not be thrown out just because the customer says so. Nevertheless, working with the customer to help them understand this is also a key point of the dialogue.

Customer centricity also means acknowledging that customers have different levels of influence over the project. Fader (2011) notes that not all customers are created equal. Fader is referring to external customers and the fact that companies should nurture regular, repeat customers. The concept still works for internal customers, though: the opinions of some stakeholders will count for more than others. Each project team will have to decide how important each project customer is. You would probably consider the views of the project sponsor as more relevant than the opinion of an interim marketing manager, who is on the periphery of the project and will be shortly replaced by a permanent employee. All feedback and all customers matter, but some matter more than others. When you have established what matters to each stakeholder, you can prioritize how these value criteria are managed. Project managers may choose to prioritize dealing with an issue raised by the project sponsor immediately, while a less important point raised by the interim marketing manager could be dealt with later. Either way, all issues are dealt with and feedback should be provided to the person who raised the point. Generally, customers are reasonable and appreciate that you cannot fix everything at once. They don't, however, appreciate being left in the dark, so if prioritization of actions is part of your strategy for being more customer-centric, be sure to build in a feedback loop so that customers know when you are planning to address their issues.

Keeping customers informed is all part of working collaboratively. In the next chapter we'll look at why collaborative project management is a step in the right direction, and explain how customer centricity builds on this.

KEY POINTS:

- Project customers are those stakeholders with a significant vested interest in the outcome of the project.
- Customer-centric project management aligns the goals of the project and the services of the project manager with the requirements and needs of the most important people on the project: the customers.
- 'Now' is the most important moment for value-driven projects.

CHAPTER 3

WHY COLLABORATIVE PROJECT MANAGEMENT IS NOT ENOUGH

Collaborative project management is where the success of the project deliverables and project management processes hinges on how teams work together. There is emphasis on knowledge sharing, cross-functional involvement, common goals, delegated authority for decisions and team ownership. The team thrives on communication and team members work in partnership with subject matter experts and the project manager to solve problems. It is the opposite of the command-and-control management model where the project manager decides the direction of the solution and plan and then directs the team to deliver to that solution.

Collaborative cultures provide a work environment that supports and motivates creative team members (Tabaka 2006). The contribution of individuals is recognized, along with the fact that one person is rarely capable of completing the project alone. Collaboration boosts the positive effect of trust and mitigates against the negative effect of conflict, creating the environment for improved performance (Chiocchio et al. 2011). Collaborative project management teams include representatives from all stakeholder groups including the customer. The acknowledgement that a strong team and teamwork are significant factors for project success (Juli 2011) has meant that collaborative working styles have become embedded in the way in which we deliver projects.

Collaborative project management is a response to changing organizational structures and working practices. Collaboration at an organizational level results in improved profits and the opportunity to access new markets (Herzog 2001). New technology, a continued desire to improve productivity and the requirement to capture organizational knowledge means that organizations are making collaboration a priority (Bicknell 2009). The command-and-control models of the past are no longer appropriate for many projects in a modern environment. Project managers, and their teams, are faced with six new challenges that cannot be adequately addressed without collaboration:

1. operating within fluid organizations
2. outsourcing

3. managing distributed teams
4. the generation gap between project team members
5. increasing project complexity
6. consumer engagement.

Let's look at each of these in turn.

CHALLENGES FOR PROJECT MANAGERS

1. Fluid Organizations

The global economic climate has not been kind to business over the early part of the twenty-first century, with issues around sub-prime debt and the single European currency. Organizations have reacted by shifting focus in order to stay solvent. Companies 'right-sized' through programmes of redundancies. Vacancies were not filled. The contractor market in some sectors was buoyant as companies were reluctant to hire permanent staff. Departments merged and split apart; non-core work was stopped or offshored and portfolios of projects were constantly reviewed, updated and changed to ensure they aligned to ever-shifting executive demands.

Project managers have to operate in this dynamic environment (Collyer et al. 2010), and become more 'hands on' with project work. Project team members may have feared for their jobs, or been given more tasks to do when colleagues were not replaced. Executive stakeholders changed, making project communication harder. Projects were cancelled or put on hold.

All of these issues required (and still require) project managers to respond to the business challenges of both fluid economic situations and shifts in the internal political landscape. This is very different to the stability of the command-and-control approaches we have seen in the past. Collaborative working involves project managers and their teams in continually redefining measures, plans, approaches and deliverables to meet these challenges.

2. Outsourcing

Organizations are becoming more reliant on outsourcing partners, partly as a response to economic turmoil. As companies choose to focus on their core competencies, outsourcing non-core work like cleaning services or IT service-desk support has become commonplace. These personnel may be based in the same location as the rest of the project team, and act as part of the host company.

As a result, project teams often include people who are not directly employed by the same company as the in-house project manager or the hiring organization of the consultant project manager.

Research from Helsinki University of Technology shows that a strong collaborative culture that includes third-party suppliers can reduce project costs and mitigate against the negative effect of project issues (Ahola 2009 cited in Dietrich et al. 2010). This research represents the upside. Our combined experience of over 30 years involvement in outsourcing has highlighted a variety of challenges for project managers reliant on outsourcer involvement. Outsource partners may be expert and specialized. They may even have empathy with the project's goals and objectives but in the final analysis, their allegiance is to their own organization and their objectives are oriented towards ensuring the relationship is profitable.

None of the principles, themes or processes of PRINCE2 (2009) discusses supplier management in detail, although procurement management is a knowledge area in *A Guide to the Project Management Body of Knowledge (PMBOK® Guide)* – 4th Edition, Project Management Institute, Inc. 2008. In a project with external suppliers, the project manager is now a supplier manager who has to contend with a foreign organization, culture and methods of operation. Outsourcers also heighten project risk, not because of any lack of competence, but because a project manager is less able to take immediate corrective action as would be possible with internal colleagues. Culture, politics, contractual limitations (not to mention pressure when projects veer off track) can lead to strained relationships and the negative effect on delivery that often comes with it.

3. Distributed Teams

Outsource partners may operate from the same location as the host company, but in many cases this does not happen. Offshoring is another business trend that has seen companies relocate offices or functions overseas to take advantage of a better supply of graduates and a more cost effective labour force.

In addition, there is growing acceptance of flexible working practices that enable employees to work from home. These can be cheaper for companies as they are not required to provide permanent office space for all employees. Flexible and home working policies cut the cost of travel, help employees manage their work/ life balance and allows companies to draw from a wider pool of employees, such as lone parents who may otherwise find it difficult to join the workforce. The UK telecoms firm BT has reported a £6–7m saving per year in operating costs as a result of flexible working practices, something that 75 per cent of employees have taken up.[1]

As a result, project managers are likely to be managing distributed or virtual teams, that is, teams that are not co-located and who collaborate at distance using technology. In a research study by ProjectsAtWork only 31 per cent of project professionals reported that their team members were in the same time zone as them. Nearly a quarter of participants reported a time difference of over nine hours. [2] Another study shows that 36 per cent of people have less than half their meetings face-to-face, with 10 per cent having no face-to-face meetings at all (Future Changes/TCW 2009).

Distributed teams of this nature may benefit from being able to maintain 24-hour working and selecting the most qualified team members for the job instead of those who happen to work locally, but global teams bring their own challenges. Project leaders have to manage cultural and language issues and collaboration across a distributed team can be more challenging.

4. The Generation Gap

'History is in the making,' write Meagan Johnson and Larry Johnson in their book, *Generations, Inc.* (2010: 217). 'Never before have five generations occupied the workplace as they do now.' Project managers (of any age) now find themselves managing multi-generational teams, and facing the challenge of creating a meaningful and rewarding work environmental for a diverse group of people motivated by very different things.

Collaboration becomes increasingly important in ensuring that team members are able to contribute effectively, and as a method of engaging younger team members in project work. Finklestein (2012) gives the example of Cisco Systems as a company that has embraced new technology – the Cisco Quad enterprise collaboration system allows employees to work together across geographies and age gaps to improve productivity and increase sales opportunities. He says that 'connection, collaboration and caring' are in the DNA of the young people who have grown up not knowing a world without the Internet.

Collaboration is hard-wired into the new recruits joining the workforce and project teams now, and to insist they set aside collaborative principles to work in the same way as their older colleagues means losing out on talent. Nearly half of employees

---

1   Mick Hegarty, Strategy and Commercial Directory, BT Business, speaking at Remote Worker Awards, London, 2010.
2   http://www.projectsatwork.com/content/White-Papers/272852.cfm [accessed: 22 April 2012].

aged 16–24 say they would not work for a company that bans access to social networking tools designed for business use. Nearly 60 per cent believe that access to social networking tools increases their effectiveness at work.[3] Collaboration is more than just social networking tools, but these statistics show that it is a key part of managing a multi-generational team.

5. Increased Project Complexity

It's not just the human dynamic that is creating a new set of challenges for project managers. Projects themselves are becoming more complex (KPMG 2005). Technology, infrastructure, regulation, legislation, changing requirements, politics, the level of change – many factors contribute to creating complex project environments. Jaafari (2003) argues that the impact of complexity on projects is so great that unless new methods are developed that allow traditional project management approaches to adapt, project managers will become irrelevant to the modern business environment.

Sauer and Reich (2009) conclude that collaboration, particularly devolved, collective decision making, is a 'practical response to complexity'. They point out that in complex projects no individual has a picture that is complete enough to enable them to make a decision alone. Collaborative project management encourages ownership, accountability and the opportunity to work collectively on problem solving, all of which are important in dealing with complex projects.

6. Consumer Engagement

The rise of social media has seen a shift in communication methods and the way that groups are organized (Harrin 2010). The web has provided more opportunities for groups to self-organize, and for individuals to vocalize complaints or issues with service providers. It also provides access to a multitude of service providers: you no longer need to buy bread from the local bakery; you can identify an artisan baker halfway across the world and have it shipped to you, if you like. Businesses have to work harder to keep customers satisfied – and reporting positive things about their experiences with them – in a world where everyone can be a journalist and brand loyalty has been eroded through choice and cost comparison.

Gamification is the art (or science) of creating consumer engagement through game-type behaviour. It is about leveraging the urge to play that is part of human nature. This can be through awarding 'badges' on user profiles on forums for a certain number of interactions, allowing consumers to rate products or services (for example, Amazon encourages customers to write book reviews, and then

3   http://www.hyphen.com/en-GB/smart-thinking/pr/Pages/GenerationFacebook.aspx [accessed: 22 April 2012].

encourages other customers to rate the reviews for helpfulness) or making special content available to those who complete quizzes, puzzles or games. Gantthead, an IT project management community website, uses badges to 'reward' contributors.[4]

Gamification has yet to make deep inroads into how projects are managed or how businesses are run but as consumer technology becomes even more advanced and incorporates elements of gamification, we are likely to see this spill over into the corporate areas, as we have seen with other consumer-adopted technology like blogs and social networking sites.

Some project management software tool vendors have already incorporated behavioural science into their products to enhance user engagement. The ability to 'like' conversation threads, which is a feature designed to encourage online collaboration and adoption in planning tool Projectplace,[5] encourages users to leave positive feedback. Positive feedback helps build trust between team members and can reduce conflict and defensive behaviour. It can also help shape behaviour, such as overcoming the barriers to the adoption of a new tool. Recipients of positive feedback find themselves going back to the tool in order to receive more positive feedback from their colleagues.[6]

Collaboration and working with consumers is recognized as a strategy to engage the people who buy or use the deliverables of a project (see for example Barefoot and Szabo 2010, Jaffe 2007) and Shenhar et al. (2002) show that customer participation is important in a project context too. Engaging internal customers in this way is an effective method of keeping close to their goals and intentions for the project. Working collaboratively also enables the project team to identify particular project customer groups that could be problematic or downright difficult and focus on these. It's the kill-them-with-kindness strategy. Successful engagement makes it harder for stakeholders to fail to participate in the project.

These six project management challenges are all underpinned by the theme of holding project team members and stakeholders together as a cohesive team, aligned to the project objectives. This common theme is why collaborative project management is a good approach for dealing with the challenges of modern projects.

Collaborative project management removes the focus on command-and-control where team members are given discrete work packages, and instead ensures that project team members have an overall, holistic view of the project and what is to be achieved. Plans and schedules are prepared with input from all the team members.

---

4   http://www.gantthead.com.
5   http://www.projectplace.com/topnav/Newsroom/Newsletter-archive/June-2011/.
6   Thanks to Mattias Hällström for his insights and commentary into behaviour shaping in project management software.

Risks and issues are mitigated and addressed through facilitative problem solving. Stakeholders are actively involved in the decision-making process instead of simply being the recipient of the deliverables at project completion, and consulting them regularly and effectively has a direct impact on project success (Khang 2008). Collaborative project management may even involve working with competitors on solutions or parts of solutions, or crowd-sourcing answers from a wide group of online volunteers. Collaborative project management creates a situation where stakeholders of all stripes including internal customers have an essential part in delivering success as part of a team working collaboratively.

A collaborative project team functions as a tight-knit unit, understanding both what they are required to do and having an input into how best to achieve it. Addressing these challenges and building a trusting, cohesive project team is now an essential part of a project manager's role. More than this, however, regular dialogue with stakeholders provides valuable feedback on how the project is going, giving the project manager early warning of potential changes and the opportunity to carry out course correction activities if required, to ensure the project, the project management team, the customer and the business objectives remain aligned. Project managers need creative ways to address these challenges and to provide a framework for constant alignment of the project team's activities with what is expected from the project stakeholders, in what could be a difficult and fast-moving organizational environment. In short, stakeholders matter.

One of the ways to address these challenges and engage stakeholders is through collaborative sharing, which Herzog (2001) has shown to be a strategic tool for project success and for building a trusting team. Collaborative sharing means taking part in the project management processes and for all parties to understand the context of the project. Herzog identifies several areas where teams can collaboratively share, including project evaluation. She recommends that project teams work with each other to develop continuous evaluation processes that can be used by project team members at all levels and at all stages throughout the project lifecycle. She also recommends that the team work collaboratively on resolving the issues that are raised as a result of continuous evaluation. Exceed is one such evaluation process.

NEXT STEPS FOR COLLABORATIVE PROJECT MANAGEMENT

Collaborative project management is an improvement on command-and-control structures. It is great that everyone has the opportunity to contribute effectively to the team, and project success (however you choose to define it – more on that in Chapter 3) is more likely with an engaged, motivated and collaborative team. But collaborative project management is not the end of the journey.

We believe that the next step for the evolution of how projects are managed is the shift to customer-centric project management. Customer-centric project management takes the premise of collaboration and enhances it to deliver something of real value to project customers.

'Customer centricity, more than anything else, is about targeting the right customers in the right way to generate the right results,' says Peter Fader in his book, *Customer Centricity* (2011: 116). Fader is discussing consumers, but the concept of customer centricity is the same in a project environment whether the customer is a colleague in a different department or someone working for a partner organization. Customer-centric project management fully involves customers in the project management process with the aim of achieving project success.

Customer-centric project management is different from 'ordinary' collaboration, because it focuses more on how things are done, as well as what things are done. Collaboration is usually a means to an end: the end of a task or project. Project teams collaborate because they know that working together is a smart option that helps them deliver more efficiently.

Customer-centric project management allows equal focus on how the delivery is happening. It is collaboration, with plenty of opportunity for process improvement and reflection along the way. That is not to say it involves navel gazing. On the contrary, putting stakeholders at the heart of the project enables a more targeted delivery of what they want, in a way that delivers real value to them. Moreover, it means that customers always know that their input is valued and that the project team is working in their interests. It allows project managers to continually redefine success measures and project deliverables in pursuit of what will always be a common goal: the successful completion of the project.

In short, collaborative project management is a set of techniques; customer-centric project management is an attitude. Even attitudes need tools to kick off, measure and record what has been achieved. In Chapter 8 we will discuss how you can implement the Exceed process to measure and manage customer centricity.

You cannot start considering the views of project customers, assessing their feedback and measuring your levels of customer centricity until you have gathered some input from them. There are a number of ways available to project managers for collecting feedback from stakeholders. Chapter 4 looks at the measures available inherent in the prevailing project management methods.

KEY POINTS:

- Collaborative project management is where the success of the project deliverables and project management processes hinge on how team members, including project customers, work together.
- Collaborative sharing is a strategic tool for project success.
- Project managers are facing new challenges that cannot be adequately addressed without collaboration: operating within fluid organizations, outsourcing, managing distributed and multi-generational teams, increasing project complexity and customer engagement.

CHAPTER 4

MEASURING PROJECT PERFORMANCE

There is a lack of consensus among practitioners and academics on the way to assess project performance and on the elusive concept of value. In this chapter we will look at current measures of project performance and explain why these approaches are no longer robust enough for projects that face the challenges mentioned in Chapter 3.

Traditionally, project performance measurement methods fall into two groups: economic and pragmatic (Aubry and Hobbs 2011). Economic measurement models are based on financial metrics and consider whether or not a project has achieved the expected financial value. Examples of economic measurement criteria are return on investment (ROI), return on capital employed (ROCE) and the use of balanced scorecards.

The challenge with these metrics is that they are all retrospective. You can forecast what you predict the ROI for your project will be (in fact you should: this will help inform the business case). However, the true cost and the true return will only be known once the project is complete, and in many cases, only several months after project completion. In complex projects operating in an environment with a fluid internal political landscape, things change fast. If ROI is a key measure you could potentially spend a lot of time recalculating your forecast in response to a fluctuating organizational environment.

Pragmatic measurement models consider elements outside economic returns. These look at whether or not a project has delivered against specified success criteria. Typically, these success criteria will be defined at the beginning of the project. When the project is in the closure phrase, these success criteria will be resurrected from a forgotten file and compared against the achievements of the project. Again, this is not practical for complex projects that may have their requirements tweaked as they progress.

With pragmatic measurement models, project managers are not encouraged to deviate from the success criteria that have been agreed at the outset. They – and the project team – are expecting to be assessed against those criteria. There is little room, if any at all, to revisit and amend the success criteria as the project progresses. These create artificial boundaries for the project manager to work within, limiting the opportunities for creative thinking and employing professional judgement to the challenges the project presents as it progresses.

While there are a number of different models to determine both success and value, there is little agreement on a clear definition of what success or value looks like in a project environment. 'There does not seem to be a particular value component that is recognized consistently from any one project management implementation or context to another,' conclude Thomas and Mullaly (2008: 301) after researching more than 65 organizations around the world. Aubry and Hobbs (2011) agree. 'There is no consensus on the way to assess either performance or the value of project management,' they report.

THE ELUSIVENESS OF 'SUCCESS'

Customer-centric project management posits that for any given project, the 'real' definition of success and value will change as that project evolves, especially in project environments addressing the challenges of fluid organizations, outsourcing, distributed and multi-generational teams, complex projects and low customer-engagement. While academics will continue to spend years debating common definitions for success and value, we ask the question: why should there be only one way to determine success?

Success means different things to different people, something that as individuals we have known and accepted in our professional, educational and family lives for years. When it comes to projects, however, researchers are keen to be able to pinpoint those elusive criteria that create 'success' or 'value,' both of which are highly subjective terms.

The fact that success varies from project to project and customer to customer is to be expected in complex organizations, as things are only 'worth' what someone thinks they are worth. Compare this to buying a house. The house is only worth what someone will pay for it. Knowledge and experience go into estimating the value, but in the end, one individual will consider a country cottage with wisteria around the door as worth more to them than a similar-sized property in a residential area close to a good school.

INTERPRETING SUCCESS CRITERIA: THE SCOTTISH PARLIAMENT PROJECT

The construction of the Scottish Parliament building is an example of how different stakeholder groups interpret success differently. Donald Dewar was Secretary of State for Scotland in 1997 as work began on the new building to house the Scottish Parliament. It was decided that an architectural competition would be held to select the design of the new building. During the announcement, Dewar commented that architectural quality, value for money, accessibility and a design 'worthy of the hopes and aspirations of the Scottish people'[1] were important. In other words, these could be interpreted as the critical success factors for the project. The contest entrants were issued with a building user brief which also stressed the importance of a stunning architectural design, saying it must 'reflect the Parliament's status', 'promote good environmental practice' and 'be an important symbol for Scotland' while offering value for money.[2] From the beginning, there was a focus on the design and the budget, and the potential for conflict between the two.

When the procurement process started, architects were bidding to deliver something within a specification of 20,740 m^2 and a budget of £50m. At this point, there were no guidelines on quality or timescale, although by the time programme plans had been produced at a strategic level, the team was forecasting a practical completion date of June 2001.

The project suffered cost over-runs and delays, and the Holyrood Inquiry, led by The Rt Hon Lord Fraser of Carmyllie, was set up to investigate. It concluded that the difficulties lay in establishing priorities. What was more important? The cost of the project, or the quality of the building? Or something else, like the delivery date or the size of the building? From the behaviour of the project team (in its widest sense), Lord Fraser concluded that actually time and quality were the two priorities, and cost was not really a concern. The procurement process had gone ahead without a realistic budget estimate.

The inquiry found that revisions to the design should have been carried out with user requirements in mind, but these were missing from the project documentation. The design team was trying to deliver something, but had no clear idea of what the client actually wanted. The principles of collaborative project management were not evident and there was no focus on customer centricity. The main problem seemed to be lack of communication. This took several forms:

---

1   http://www.scottish.parliament.uk/SPICeResources/HolyroodInquiry.pdf page 51 [accessed: 22 April 2012].
2   http://www.scottish.parliament.uk/Audio_files/Building_User_Brief.pdf [accessed: 22 April 2012].

- Messages were filtered for political reasons before being passed on to management. For example, a quantity surveyor produced an estimate of £89m, including a margin in case of risk; after all, this was a one-of-a-kind project, and it was highly likely there would be some unforeseen circumstances. The actual estimate passed up the line did not include this risk prediction, and was given as £62m. It is possible that the person passing the information up the line saw adherence to budget as one of the key criteria for this project.
- Unclear vocabulary used in project reports. Terminology (project management jargon and all other business vocabularies) only works when everyone using it has a common understanding of what it means. Is 'estimate' the same as 'forecast'? The misunderstandings (whether intentional or not) that this uncommon vocabulary had on the team did not help advance the project and may have led to different groups having different views about what the project was actually going to deliver.
- Absence of project reports. There were concerns over whether or not the project would be completed within budget as early as November 1998. However, it took until March 1999 before Donald Dewar was given formal warning of any potential cost rise. If budget was a key success criterion for the project, it seems it was not communicated adequately to those responsible for reporting against it – or they were providing the information to the wrong stakeholders.
- Lack of general communication at all levels. The project manager, Bill Armstrong, led the project until December 1998. He then resigned, but the senior stakeholders were not aware of his departure until it was covered in the media in January 1999. This is symptomatic of the way in which the overall relationships worked between the stakeholders on this project.

The Members of the Scottish Parliament met in their new building for the first time in September 2004 – three years after the initial planned practical completion date. If delivery date was a measure of success for this construction programme, it certainly failed. Businesses in the locale suffered disruption for longer than expected during the build and Members of the Scottish Parliament who expected to be sitting in their new building three years prior could have seen the delays as an inconvenience and the construction project as a failure.

The cost of the building rose significantly from the initial figure quoted in the procurement process. In 2004 the estimated final cost reported to the Finance Committee was £431m. Value for money is inherently subjective, but it is clear that if cost was a measure of success for this construction programme, the debate between project team members about whether success was achieved would go on late into the night.

However, the building had attracted 100,000 visitors by November that year.[3] It has won nine design awards.[4] The three main parts of the building have been rated as 'excellent' for environmental performance and the development has increased biodiversity in the area.[5] The carbon footprint of the Holyrood complex has been reduced by 12 per cent in 5 years.[6] It is clear that the success criteria of accessibility, stunning design and good environmental practice have been met. To the local community who visited the building, the architectural community who have praised it and the citizens who benefit from the decreasing impact the building has on the environment, the project has succeeded.

Project success looks different to different project stakeholders.

THE PROBLEM OF POST-IMPLEMENTATION REVIEWS

Not every project has a full-scale public inquiry to assess how the deliverables turned out. The vehicle for determining success in most cases is the post-implementation review (PIR), also known as a project post-mortem or post-project review. This is often the only opportunity to assess success, although some organizations adopt a more robust method of benefits tracking.

There are two issues with PIRs: they only happen at the end of projects and they mainly focus on the project management principles and methods used. They don't make the distinction between the success of the project and the success of the project management effort, and they mainly focus on the latter.

'Postmortems are the central mechanism for continual improvement of project processes,' writes Moore (2010). 'Without a feedback mechanism, such as a postmortem, any process improvement is little more than informed guesswork … If you are using a workflow to underpin projects, the postmortem should be one of the final steps in that workflow.'

Whether you call the meeting a PIR, a post-mortem or a post-project review, the thing that all the terms have in common is the word 'post'.[7] In other words,

---

3   See http://www.scottish.parliament.uk/visitandlearn/16333.aspx [accessed: 22 April 2012].
4   See http://www.scottish.parliament.uk/visitandlearn/16187.aspx [accessed: 22 April 2012].
5   See http://www.scottish.parliament.uk/visitandlearn/18794.aspx [accessed: 22 April 2012].
6   See http://www.scottish.parliament.uk/visitandlearn/15065.aspx [accessed: 22 April 2012].
7   We particularly take issue with the term 'post-mortem': it's difficult to disassociate the word from death in suspicious or unexpected circumstances and there's an undertone of project failure.

they come after the project has completed, or very near the end. Atkinson (1999) even argues that you should delay assessing success until well after the project is completed, so that the longer-term benefits can be included in the discussion.

Sometimes customers will be asked to feed into the project evaluation process (Littau et al. 2010), but at that point it is too late to do anything practical about their comments. If they complain that they weren't kept up to date, you cannot go back in time and provide more information on a regular basis. It is a case of, 'How can I help you now it is too late?' In fact, research from South Africa shows that project sponsors prefer a proactive approach to feedback over the PIR process. They chose to work collaboratively with the project manager during the project to ensure that their expectations were met (Sewchurran and Barron 2008).

Another team of academics from the UK, Norway and Australia carried out a research project in 2009 into the early warning signs that indicate that complex projects are going off course. 'Post-project review and assessment cannot change what has already happened and hence does not provide any useful early warning signal to the completed project,' comment Klakegg et al. (2010). They also conclude that 'human concerns can be a valuable source of early warning signals' and advocate for discussions with stakeholders to uncover issues around the project's health. A customer-centric approach builds on this by making these discussions a regular part of stakeholder engagement, even if the team is split across many locations.

Of course, PIR discussions are immensely valuable for continuous process improvement, and we are not advocating that you stop using this technique. Focusing on project management principles and methods used is essential to improve organizational project management processes. Could we have done better risk management? What scheduling lessons were learned? A good PIR meeting should discuss what went well and what did not go so well with this project. However, this approach takes the customer, and often outsourcing partners, out of the equation. There is no room in the process improvement discussion for whether the project team delivered a result that the customer thought was valuable, regardless of the processes used, or whether they were satisfactorily engaged throughout the project lifecycle.

Aside from the process topics during a PIR, it is also an opportunity to discuss statistics and metrics related to the project. If PIR discussions do include metrics, these are normally backward-looking. What was the percentage of effort spent on testing? How many days did it take the quality team to audit the deliverables? These metrics and calculations can then be incorporated into future projects so that initiatives going forward have the benefit of experience and hindsight. However, that doesn't help the project customer of this particular project. The 'now' moment – the moment that the customer most cares about – is over for their project. The customer's role in post-project discussions is simply to help you improve your working practices so that other people can benefit. And in many cases the minutes from the PIR meeting are filed away and never looked at again. Nobody benefits from this kind of routine post-mortem, as the organizational knowledge is not appropriately shared.

Customer-centric project management helps your current customer to benefit from incremental, tailored improvements to the project along the way, and it can be done alongside traditional post-mortem meetings. We will see an example of how this works in practice in Chapter 6.

BEYOND THE PIR: DEFINING SUCCESS DIFFERENTLY

'There is no unequivocal definition of project success,' writes Wake (2008). 'Cost, schedule, specification are often used to declare it. Think about it. This isn't success, it's compliance. If you want success, then it is normally expressed in the opinions of yourself, your peers, subordinates or bosses, but not necessarily at all levels at the same time.' We could spend a lot of time debating success criteria. In fact, many academics already have. The definition of project success has widened over the years. Geoghegan (2008), Dvir et al. (1998), White and Fortune (2002), Hyväri (2006), Shenhar and Dvir (2007) and others have all undertaken insightful research into success criteria. However, we share the view of Herzog (2001) that the definition of success is a variable defined by the person you interview.

As we saw, the PIR process can include both the discussion of successes and failures (euphemistically called deltas at some of the places we have worked) as well as project metrics. In our experience, it is rare for customer satisfaction to be one of those metrics, but we believe it should be. To the customer at least, nothing else matters. Therefore we need a framework to help define what value and success looks like to an individual project customer, and a way to consistently measure that and provide worthwhile metrics on an ongoing basis.

The idea of caring about and measuring customer satisfaction is not new. As we have seen, other industries have done this for some time. There is already some movement towards incorporating customer satisfaction metrics into project management. These metrics include measuring return business, the management of controlled disruption, adherence to quality standards and number of customer objectives met (Bowles 2011). These are good measures but they mainly focus on the consumers who buy the end product. Dvir et al. (1998), Atkinson (1999) and Shenhar and Dvir (2007) have discussed customer satisfaction as a criterion for project success, and Zhai et al. (2009) discuss its positive contribution to the perception of project management value. The *PMBOK® Guide* (2008) defines the success of projects as product and project quality, timeliness, budget compliance and 'degree of customer satisfaction'. We assume that these are internal customers, although it provides no further guidance on how to establish or assess customer satisfaction. *Managing Successful Projects with PRINCE2™* (2009) says that a key success factor is that the user finds the deliverable acceptable, but concludes that the only way to do this is to be clear up front about expectations on both sides so that success can be assessed at the end.

This is the fundamental problem: customers do not assess success at the end. They assess it as they participate in the project lifecycle, in their 'now' moments. All the talk of measuring customer satisfaction is a step in the right direction, but until project management takes on board the fact that customers do not assess success in the same way that we do, the methodologies available will continue to advocate using metrics that are only available at the end of the project, and therefore cannot contribute to shaping the project management effort.

Working with the new paradigm of customer-centric project management means accepting that levels of satisfaction change as opportunities and risks present themselves during the project lifecycle. Assessing customer satisfaction only at the end of the project is not adequate.

The Exceed process, as we will see in the next chapter, helps teams define success for internal customers so that they can act in a more customer-centric way. Project customers are the group that needs to be happy before the end product ever gets to a consumer.

KEY POINTS:

- 'Value' can be an elusive commodity.
- Success is a variable defined by the people you ask, when you ask them.
- Collaborative project management is not enough to deliver a successful result in an environment where the definition of success is not limited to measures of time, cost and quality.
- PIRs and project post-mortems focus more on process, and less on what was delivered.
- Customer satisfaction is rarely assessed during a PIR, and even if it is, this retrospective view is not adequate. Customer-centric project managers should accept that satisfaction levels change as opportunities and risks present themselves during the project.

CHAPTER 5

CUSTOMER CENTRICITY IN PRACTICE: A CASE STUDY

In the summer of 2007 the well-known health insurance company Bupa sold its network of private hospitals to Spire Healthcare, a new company backed by venture capital group Cinven. Whilst Bupa Hospitals was an extremely well-known brand, private hospitals represented only 11 per cent of Bupa's overall business.

Since the acquisition, Spire has achieved an impressive record of success. At time of writing (October 2011) the company was the third-fastest growing company in the UK and reported earnings before interest, depreciation and amortization of £169.8m. Spire now employs 7,500 people in its network of independent hospitals.

In terms of IT, Spire faced a 'green field' situation. The new company owned virtually no IT equipment and had no data centre. Only a handful of IT staff transferred as part of the sale process.

An IT services partner was selected and tasked with delivering most of the service management elements including the service desk, machine hosting, technical infrastructure support and networking. They also provided some infrastructure IT project management services. The internal Spire IT team comprised a small applications support group, a small team of in-house project managers and a service delivery team responsible for infrastructure strategy, supplier management, security and customer care. The team was distributed across several locations. This department, together with the outsourcing partner, was responsible for getting all the new IT services up and running for the new company.

The team knew that the successful transition away from Bupa relied on a clean and smooth IT handover. The only way to do this was to keep internal customers informed of what was going on and involve them every step of the way. Success required a customer-centric approach. Having adopted customer centricity as a core value of how the team worked, they needed to implement a way to measure and monitor this during the transition.

Led by the service delivery team, the Exceed process was implemented across all the hospital and central functions. There are eight steps required to set up and implement Exceed, and the team worked through them all in turn. The steps taken were:

1. Support for the vision: obtain buy in from the ultimate authority.
2. Educate the organization: spread the vision.
3. Decide who the customer is.
4. Define a simple scoring mechanism which customers can use to rate the services they receive.
5. Organize for success.
6. Align service partners.
7. Launch the Exceed process.
8. Deliver on the issues.

Let's look at each of those steps in detail, and how the team put the process into action.

STEP 1: SUPPORT FOR THE VISION: OBTAIN BUY IN FROM THE ULTIMATE AUTHORITY

Customer centricity was first adopted in service delivery and was later extended to the project management function. Spire CIO Marc O'Brien embraced this way of working from day one, despite having a healthy degree of scepticism as to whether a significant-sized customer base across over 40 locations, used to receiving a relatively poor IT service, could be convinced to return scores of Good, Very Good or Excellent for his emerging regime. There is no organization more fluid than one going through a merger, acquisition or separation and the transition work presented huge operational challenges.

While Marc's position was understandable, he was also in agreement with the overriding principles of customer centricity: that customers were everything, that Spire IT would engage with them comprehensively using the Exceed process and that their needs would come first. These aims may sound obvious, but this approach represented a major shift within a function which had been considered faceless, unresponsive and unapproachable.

STEP 2: EDUCATE THE ORGANIZATION: SPREAD THE VISION

The Spire IT service delivery functional responsibilities are laid out in Figure 5.1.

IT Service Delivery Functions

Function	Customer Management	Technical Infrastructure Management and Security	Service Management	Service Integration
Vision:	To deliver IT Services to all Spire business areas which are rated as good, very good or excellent	To provide technical architecture which is resilient, technically fit for purpose, proactively managed and value for money Network / Midrange / Presentation / Voice	To deliver high quality IT services in conjunction with valued service partners	To seamlessly manage the integration of project based initiatives into the service delivery environment
Plan	Understand business requirements Keep customer management processes under constant review	Research market Stay with current thinking Evaluate and present options Look for innovation which offers business value Present business cases Hold technical infrastructure strategy plans	Maintain services portfolio Keep operational/delivery processes under constant review Interface internally to gain full understanding of proposed change strategy and its effect on service delivery	Obtain early warning of issues, projects which potentially affect the ability of IM&T to maintain or enhance service levels Manage the project portfolio in terms of process ownership and status reporting
Design	Identify service improvement options Identify multiple user contact strategies and methods which reflect business importance/benefits derived Interface with internal functions to gain early warning of plans and changes which affect customers	Own technical designs Build in resilience and security Own configuration information and diagrams. Create standards framework necessary to Manage security accreditations Create a technical roadmap for infrastructure development	Agree service delivery methods/ standards with partners to maintain quality /maximise value Implement service improvement strategies Integrate internal roles into service processes (change, problem escalation	Design and maintain IM&T Portfolio Management process from inception to integration Create effective processes for interfacing with internal functions and stakeholders engaged in project activity
Operate	Act as prime customer interface for customer care Own every customer related service issue Manage "Exceed Programme" which delivers satisfaction rating of good, very good or excellent Prime customer interface for service change, interruptions, projects and implementations	Support Exceed process and activities Actively monitor performance of technical environment with service partners Input to relationship management with service partners and technical suppliers Approve technical changes Interface in problem situations Assist in new developments and projects monitor costs Prepare budgets in line with business and technical plans Maintain and monitor security processes	Support Exceed process and activities Prime interface with service delivery partners Manage service levels Manage risk/reward process Agree additional costs Give final change management approval Manage enhancement request process including new IT purchases Monitor new services into production Manage service delivery budgets	Prime interface for IM&T, service partners and business based resources engaged in project activity which affects service delivery Marshall correct service delivery and partner resources in support of business cases and projects Own service delivery project plans thereby enabling service delivery resources to focus on specific actions and technical input

Figure 5.1 IT Service Delivery Functions

This schematic was used to make clear to the entire IT organization that the customer services function (the left section) would act as the principle customer interface. This function would own all issues through to resolution. A clear expectation was set that each IT function, including those provided by the IT project managers and partners, would be lined up in support of that area as it brought issues to the table.

STEP 3: DECIDE WHO THE CUSTOMER IS

Spire's business is private healthcare delivered through a network of 38 hospitals stretched throughout the UK from Edinburgh to Southampton. Each hospital is run by a hospital director with an individual profit target and full profit and loss responsibility. The performance of each hospital was vitally important for Spire's overall business results, as were the key supporting functions: logistics centres in the North, Midlands and South, the finance department in Manchester and a central London head office which provided other support and central functions such as marketing and legal services. It was decided to measure IT performance against all of them individually. Exceed would cover over 40 sites and be run by a distributed team, for a distributed team.

STEP 4: DEFINE A SIMPLE SCORING MECHANISM WHICH CUSTOMERS CAN USE TO RATE THE SERVICES THEY RECEIVE

Likert scales, named after Rensis Likert, who developed this method of scoring in 1932, are used to establish the extent to which someone agrees or disagrees with a statement. They are often used in questionnaires. Likert scales ask respondents to indicate their response to the statement by identifying a number in a range. Common scales use a 5- or 7-point range, but Spire chose to adapt a 10-point scale. The measures used are shown in Table 5.1.

By consistently using the same scale across all customer groups, a picture could be built up of the organization as a whole. This set of diagnostic metrics would provide real-time information about the levels of customer satisfaction with IT services across the business.

Table 5.1   Rating scale used for measuring customer satisfaction levels

Score	Description
10	Excellent
9	Consistently Very Good
8	Very Good
7	Consistently Good
6	Good
5	Acceptable
4	Poor
3	Consistently Poor
2	Very Poor
1	Consistently Very Poor

STEP 5: ORGANIZE FOR SUCCESS

Three Customer Services Managers (CSMs) were recruited with a brief to engage with each hospital on a face-to-face basis at least once every month in order to gain first-hand information on their requirements and issues – a kind of relationship audit.[1] The CSMs were selected more for their personal qualities than any technical ability. None of them had first-hand experience of the workings of hospital businesses but all were highly customer-focused individuals with excellent communication skills and a real desire to deliver a quality result. Their brief was to take ownership of their allocated group of 10–15 business units and start the process of engagement. This involved each CSM spending an average of four days a week on the road: a distributed and mobile team focusing on customer satisfaction.

A new position was established within the department to collate the output from these meetings and to monitor the resolution of issues against targets once the process was fully underway. The internal IT functions were reminded of the need to respond promptly to anything labelled as an issue raised through the Exceed process.

---

1   The authors are indebted to Kevin Murray for this term. K. Murray, 2011, *The Language of Leaders*, London: Kogan Page, p. 95

STEP 6: ALIGN SERVICE PARTNERS

The IT department was working with partners through a number of outsourcing agreements. Service partners were fully briefed about the Exceed process and the new focus on the customer. A scale of monthly incentive payments directly relating to customer satisfaction ratings was agreed with some partners where this was appropriate.

STEP 7: LAUNCH THE EXCEED PROCESS

At the first visit, the CSMs delivered a 15-minute presentation to each of their allotted business units outlining our interest in customer satisfaction and the aims of the Exceed process. They offered themselves as a point of contact for any IT issues a customer had. They also committed to discussing issues and challenges on a monthly basis. As Zhai et al. (2009) acknowledge, stakeholders have different needs at different times and in different contexts. We wanted to reassure the hospital teams that the engagement would be there over the long term, regardless of how the internal landscape of the organization changed during the transition away from Bupa.

Hospital directors and their management teams were eager to engage given the criticality of IT to their operations. The CSMs were welcomed warmly by customers who had never seen a person from IT in the flesh.

Discussions with the first few hospitals resulted in four measurement areas which were then accepted by each business unit as the standard by which IT's performance would be rated. These were:

- how well IT managed their top three issues;
- how well IT communicates;
- how proactive IT is perceived to be;
- how they would rate general levels of IT service quality.

A simple spreadsheet was produced to act as a template for the monthly conversations and to record the output from the customer on a regular basis. Once the scores were captured, the results would be published monthly on the intranet. The transparency of recording and publishing the results was important to show that the team was serious about the process and committed to resolving issues. This also helped those team members in remote locations, including some customers themselves, access the data in timely fashion. The intranet site was not available to third-party partners, but the scores were also shared with them as appropriate.

The first formal Exceed scores recorded in May 2008 were unsurprisingly well below our target of Good, Very Good or Excellent but already they reflected the effect of the initial contacts made throughout the entire Spire estate. Average scores at this time are shown in Table 5.2.

Table 5.2   Average customer satisfaction scores from May 2008

Measurement area	Score
Management of top issues	3.55 (Consistently Poor to Poor)
Communication	5.24 (Acceptable)
Proactivity	5.03 (Acceptable)
Service quality	4.59 (Poor)
Average customer satisfaction in major business centres (Head Office, HR, Finance, Legal, Marketing)	6.19 (Good)
Average customer satisfaction in hospitals/logistics centres	4.60 (Poor)

These were interesting results and represented the first evidence of customer perceptions of the new IT organization. Given that some customers had never before seen a person from IT, the Exceed process itself undoubtedly contributed to receiving a score of Acceptable for communication and proactivity. The historically poor level of service came through in poor scores for the vital areas of managing top issues (although the process had only just begun) and overall service quality.

There was some good news though. Important corporate functions (HR, finance, legal and marketing) were happy with IT, rating the service as Good.

STEP 8: DELIVER ON THE EXCEED RESULTS

After the first round of meetings it quickly became apparent that there was much to be done and that customer satisfaction with the levels of IT service could be significantly improved. It was clear that the IT organization would be judged on its response to the points and issues raised during this initial round of discussions. After all, while customers appreciated the opportunity to air their views about the quality of IT, they really wanted to see their problems resolved and their concerns addressed.

Knowing that this would be the case, the team had undertaken a month of informal engagement prior to the formal launch of the process and this had seen some problems resolved on first contact. The CSM allocated to the head office functions worked hard to resolve issues in what was a less complex environment than hospitals.

More than 180 customer inputs were recorded in the month after the formal launch. The issues were wide ranging, as can be seen from this sample:

- Site has been waiting on a couple of purchase requests for some time.
- Printer in marketing is still not fixed; waiting on a replacement part. This issue has been ongoing for about three weeks.
- Faulty PC will not boot up.
- Telephony issues are causing major problems within hospital.
- Server on site is not backing up correctly.
- It took the radiology manager 32 minutes to get through to the service desk yesterday. This is a regular occurrence.

A longer sample of the list from that time has been reproduced in Appendix 1 in order to illustrate the nature of issues any organization is likely to face when beginning to truly listen to what is important to customers. Needless to say, identifying these issues was the first step in being able to put them right.

ANALYSING THE RESULTS

At first glance, a list of 180 issues to resolve – some relating to projects, some related to business as usual – represents a daunting list of concerns. In fact, when analysing the detail we see a mixture of problems but many common threads: service desk performance, computer problems, purchasing delays, general lack of responsiveness. One comment from a hospital indicated almost a sense of puzzlement at being asked to score IT in terms of proactivity.

However, there was much that was encouraging in the comments that were recorded. Most, if not all, of the issues raised were fixable given the necessary focus and determination.

Now that the whole IT team knew what was really important to customers, real operational changes were made. Our outsource partner was fully brought on board and commissioned to supply a team of mobile field engineers. These engineers 'adopted' groups of hospitals in much the same way as the CSMs had done. Customers got to know their dedicated engineer. Now there was someone who could quickly get to the business unit, who knew his way around and who could assist in the moves, changes and technical projects which affected his site. The service desk was also reorganized to be more responsive, and internal processes were revised or replaced.

Analysis by business unit showed that some were happier than others. Some had fewer than half a dozen issues. Some were pleased with the level of communication and proactivity shown by IT in seeking requirements for projects. All had needs and concerns which were clear and unquestionable.

This was the starting point for our move to a more customer-centric approach. We worked on the basis that clarity leads to understanding; understanding leads to confidence, and confidence, together with determination, would produce a clear and positive result.

ADDRESSING THE ISSUES

Customer centricity had arrived. Spire's IT organization went to work on knocking down these issues. Within two months all scores of Poor had been eliminated. Within a further two months all scores were at least Good or well on the way to being Good. By the fifth month, all scores were between Good and Consistently Good. Since then, customer satisfaction has continued to rise steadily. Figure 5.2 shows the improvement over time.

THE SITUATION TODAY

As we've seen, the initial list of issues contained more than 180 items. Further examination concluded that many were duplicate issues experienced by multiple customer areas and which could be solved by applying generic solutions. Many were trivial, others the more challenging results of an organization going through a major change. A junior service manager's role was refocused to include responsibility for chasing down resolutions. This person had great communication skills, an overwhelming desire to look after customers and wouldn't take no for an answer. Within 6 months there were only 12 outstanding issues.

Spire IT's appetite for customer centricity has never diminished. Recent Exceed reviews highlight only a few service issues. When issues do emerge, as they always will in a dynamic, complex and constantly changing operating environment, they are tackled immediately as the priority is always to protect and improve customer satisfaction ratings. The snapshot of overall satisfaction from the time of writing is shown in Figure 5.3.

As you can see, there are 73 scores of Excellent included in this impressive set of ratings.

Master Exceed scores from May 2008 to Oct 2011

May 2008 to Oct 2011	May-08	Nov-08	May-09	Nov-09	May-10	Nov-10	May-11	Oct-11
Top Three Issues	3.65	7.00	7.05	8.78	8.89	9.05	9.32	9.29
Communication	5.24	7.17	7.64	8.73	8.89	8.81	8.89	8.92
Proactivity	5.03	7.24	7.59	8.84	9.00	9.03	9.11	9.16
Service Quality	4.69	7.00	7.56	8.70	8.73	8.49	8.89	8.89
Average Customer Satisfaction	5.40	7.00	7.76	9.03	8.96	8.90	9.15	9.11
Average Service Rating: Major Business Centres	6.19	6.90	8.05	9.30	9.05	8.95	9.25	9.15
Average Service Rating: Hospitals and Supply Chain	4.60	7.10	7.46	8.76	8.88	8.84	9.05	9.07

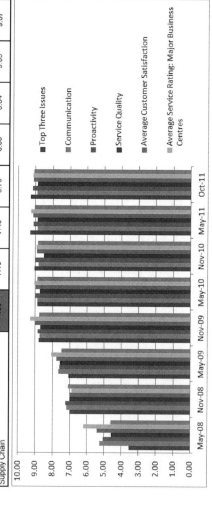

Figure 5.2 Exceed scores in IT service delivery between May 2008 and October 2011

Exceed Customer Satisfaction Record (October 2011)

Average Customer Satisfaction:	Consistently Very Good	9.20

Summary of Key Business Areas

Average service rating: Major Business Centres	Consistently Very Good	9.20
Average service rating: Hospitals and NDC	Consistently Very Good - For Hospitals	9.20

Supporting Individual Measures

Major Business Centres	Top 3 issues	Communication	Proactivity	Service Quality	Average
Head Office: Legal & Finance	10	9	9	9	9.25
Head office: Marketing & Business Improvement	10	10	10	10	10.00
Head Office: CEO	10	10	10	10	10.00
Head Office: HR	10	10	10	10	10.00
Hospital Support Centre	6	7	7	7	6.75
Average Rating	**9.20**	**9.20**	**9.20**	**9.20**	**9.20**

Hospitals and National Distribution Centre	Top 3 issues	Communication	Proactivity	Service Quality	Average
Alexandra	10	10	10	10	10.00
Bristol	10	10	10	10	10.00
Bushey	10	10	10	8	9.50
Cambridge Lea	10	9	9	9	9.25
Cardiff	10	9	9	10	9.50
Clare Park	10	9	9	9	9.25
Dunedin	8	9	9	9	8.75
Edinburgh/Shawfair	9	9	9	9	9.00
Elland	10	9	10	8	9.25
Fylde Coast	9	9	8	8	8.50
Gatwick	9	9	10	10	9.50
Harpenden	10	10	10	10	10.00
Hartswood	9	8	8	8	8.25
Hull and East Riding	9	9	9	9	9.00
Leeds	10	6	10	7	8.25
Leicester	9	10	10	9	9.50
Little Aston	10	10	9	9	9.50
Liverpool	10	9	10	10	9.75
London Fertility Clinic	6	8	8	7	7.25
Manchester	9	9	9	9	9.00
Methley Park	10	9	9	9	9.25
NDC	9	9	8	7	8.25
Cheshire	10	9	10	10	9.75
Norwich	8	8	9	8	8.25
Parkway	10	10	10	10	10.00
Portsmouth	9	9	9	9	9.00
Regency	4	10	9	10	8.25
Roding	10	9	9	10	9.50
South Bank	10	9	9	8	9.00
Sussex	10	10	10	10	10.00
Southampton	10	9	9	9	9.25
St Saviours	8	9	9	9	8.75
Thames Valley	10	10	10	10	10.00
Tunbridge Wells	10	10	10	10	10.00
Washington	9	9	10	9	9.25
Wellesley	9	9	9	10	9.25
Wirral	10	9	9	10	9.50
Yale (Wrexham)	10	9	9	10	9.50
Average Rating	**9.29**	**9.13**	**9.29**	**9.11**	**9.20**

Key

10. Excellent
9. Consistently Very Good
8. Very Good
7. Consistently Good
6. Good
5. Acceptable
4. Poor
3. Consistently Poor
2. Consistently Poor
1. Consistently Very Poor

Figure 5.3   Consolidated customer satisfaction scores for Spire Healthcare as at October 2011

After the success of Exceed in a service delivery environment, we turned our attention to delivering the same level of customer satisfaction and engagement across projects, and that is discussed in more detail in the next chapter.

KEY POINTS:

- Customer centricity is a mindset; engagement to this approach is key at all levels.
- Use a simple process to record, measure and monitor satisfaction levels.
- Keep satisfaction scoring criteria as simple as possible.
- Deliver on your promises.
- Ensure that outsourcing partners and other third parties are fully included: they are also important for gaining customer satisfaction.
- A focus on specifics delivers the most value to customers.

CHAPTER 6

CUSTOMER CENTRICITY IN A PROJECT ENVIRONMENT

'Getting the voice of the customer is critical in process improvement and the PMO should constantly be trying to improve and increase its value to the organization,' writes Peter Taylor in his book, *Leading Successful PMOs* (2011: 61). 'They need to relate to their customers/users, involve them in decisions and communicate with them often.'

At Spire Healthcare, the IT project managers acknowledged that the voice of the customer was improving service in other areas of IT, as we saw in the previous chapter. Customers were receiving proactive solicitation of feedback and having their operational IT issues resolved, and after two years of engaging with IT in this way, it felt strangely archaic not to have the same level of engagement with IT projects.

In addition, the project managers were dealing with many of the operational 'new world' challenges we discussed in Chapter 3. The organization had gone through many iterations of change since the separation from Bupa, including creating a PMO function, revising all the project management processes and refocusing efforts on a portfolio of projects to meet the needs of the new company. In addition, advances in medical technology were creating the need for ever more complex projects and networking solutions.

The fledgling PMO accepted the fact that the traditional approach of waiting until the end of the project to gather feedback from the customer to input into the post-implementation review was not providing the team with the possibility of acting as proactively as they would like. There was a desire to further improve the project methodology to adapt to some of these challenges but it was difficult to know where to start with gathering the voice of the customer.

While the team was keen to adopt a more customer-centric approach, there was scepticism about how best to do this. Why would a process that worked for the business-as-usual operational side of IT work for projects which are by their nature transient and which use temporary teams? 'If you think about it,' write Shenhar and

Dvir in their book, *Reinventing Project Management* (2007: 3), 'every operational process began as a project that put things in motion.' This is the link between IT service delivery and IT projects, and it is not surprising that operations led the way for process improvement. After all, over the years developments like Lean, Six Sigma and supply chain management have rapidly improved efficiency at an operational level (Shenhar and Dvir 2007).

The challenge of using the Exceed process with projects was that they often didn't last long enough to gather meaningful monthly data. At the start of the project nothing much had happened for the project customer to comment about. By the time it was over, a post-implementation review would give us some useful information. In between, would the project last long enough for us to improve processes or resolve issues so that we would see an improvement in scores?

We were also concerned about overloading customers with their monthly visit about overall IT service from their CSM and then having to do the same process for projects. This was especially problematic in some business areas where we were delivering more than one IT project at a time. Senior stakeholders in each business area were often the same for both general IT issues and projects. Would customers get survey fatigue?

Where the project customers were not the same individuals whom the CSM met monthly, they were often clinical staff. This presented another problem. Clinical team members – nurses, physiotherapists, radiographers and so on – all had a day job to do treating patients. IT projects were a means to an end, and while clinical staff did form an active and essential part of project teams, asking for more of their time away from patients to complete surveys for us felt like a poor use of their valuable time. Would they be willing to give up time to help us improve our project delivery, and would the project managers be willing to ask for it?

During 2010 we found a way to address all of these concerns.

Spire was undergoing a £multi-million IT hardware and software programme to upgrade the technology in the radiology departments of all the hospitals. This was a four-year programme, and 2010 was the final year. The work tabled for that year involved projects to install the new system at eight hospitals, deliver a central software upgrade and replace some IT and medical technology hardware. The length of the programme meant that even if individual projects did not last more than a couple of months, overall the programme would benefit from gathering customer feedback and acting on it. The core programme team was split across five locations and was also travelling extensively to different hospitals and offices as required. We thought that the output from the Exceed process would allow us to standardize our approach across a distributed team and effectively share the best practices from each individual project.

We also agreed to start out by rotating the Exceed survey amongst project customers, so that while the programme would get a regular supply of Exceed feedback to act on, individual project customers would not feel overloaded with a request to participate in yet one more meeting.

Service delivery had done much of the groundwork over the previous two years, and the project managers and business units were aware of the ideas and benefits behind this customer-centric approach. As a result, we were able to skip Step 1 of the implementation process. We moved straight to Step 2.

STEP 2: EDUCATE THE ORGANIZATION: SPREAD THE VISION

While the IT service delivery function had been working in a customer-centric way for some time, the project management team had been doing so only informally. The shift to the mindset of customer-centric project management was not a difficult one to make. The shift to introducing the Exceed process to facilitate the engagement and document the outcome was slightly harder, as this was an extra task for project managers to take on. However, the team was positive about using Exceed as a tool for better customer engagement on projects.

STEP 3: DECIDE WHO THE CUSTOMER IS

The programme team agreed that while we were trialling the Exceed process in a project environment the customers would be the individual with the most to gain from that project. The project sponsor was often the hospital director, but the person who was most impacted by the project deliverables on this programme was the diagnostic imaging manager, and this was the individual we targeted for Exceed reviews. This enabled us to set credible, realistic expectations on both sides.

STEP 4: DEFINE A SIMPLE SCORING MECHANISM WHICH CUSTOMERS CAN USE TO RATE THE SERVICES THEY RECEIVE

There are three types of project metrics: predictive, diagnostic and retrospective. Diagnostic metrics allow the project manager and other interested stakeholders to track progress. They can also act as early warning signs and triggers for decision-making and problem-solving (Kendrick 2012). The PMO decided that the 10-point Likert scale in use in service delivery was a simple diagnostic metric that would provide progress information, so this was maintained. This had the benefit of ensuring that there was one consistent explanation of Good, Very Good and Excellent for all the Exceed reviews done across IT and the rest of the business.

The programme manager took the questions from the Exceed spreadsheet in use in service delivery, but after reviewing them decided that they were not appropriate for a project environment. The flexibility of Exceed meant that the programme team could define their own measures. For this programme, the measures chosen were:

- how well the project team managed issues;
- how well the project team communicated;
- how well the project deliverables are being integrated into the existing hospital processes;
- how well the project is going overall.

The question around integration was particularly important to this programme as the team was also key in managing the business change through co-ordinating training, process mapping and re-engineering, and supporting the clinical and administrative users through the shift in working practices to adopt the new technology.

These questions were all naturally subjective measures, but subjective opinion was what we wanted to understand.

STEP 5: ORGANIZE FOR SUCCESS

It quickly became apparent that the success of these conversations with project customers would be heavily dependent on the person leading the discussion. Service delivery had created the role of the CSM to facilitate these discussions and to own any resulting issues through to closure. Project managers were now expected to do the same. However, only one of the project managers had a customer service background, and as a team they were not properly equipped to have this level of conversation. This was addressed in several ways.

First, the existing template spreadsheet from service delivery was amended to reflect the new measures. This was built into the project management process and the reviews were carried out in routine project meetings. This was different to the way CSMs gathered their customer satisfaction metrics, which was typically during a dedicated, face-to-face meeting solely for the purpose of discussing IT services. Project managers sometimes gathered their results over the phone. This was a direct response to making the best use of the hospital team's time, and making the questions feel like less of a burden to both the clinical and programme team members.

Second, project managers were given the opportunity to shadow CSMs to see how they managed the conversations.

Third, the programme manager decided that the project managers needed to be fully aware of the commitment and executive engagement in this shift to a customer-centric way of working. The template for the monthly departmental report to the executive management team was rewritten to include a placeholder for customer satisfaction scores for the month. Each project manager's personal objectives, which were tied to the possibility of earning a bonus as part of the annual review process, were amended to include the objective of achieving scores of Consistently Good or better. This was agreed as a realistic target for the first year of measuring satisfaction levels.

STEP 6: ALIGN SERVICE PARTNERS

Projects and programmes do not happen in a vacuum, and this programme was certainly no different. We had a third-party vendor providing the software and some hardware for the solution. As the four-year programme involved a rolling deployment of a new system to hospitals, some hospitals received their services long before the programme was finished. As a result, we were managing both a solution in operation and new deployments.

Monthly meetings were held with the vendor where project issues and any other issues were discussed. In effect, we turned the customer-centric approach around and the programme manager became the customer of services from the vendor. The vendor was scored monthly on the service they were providing, using the same Exceed spreadsheet. This helped both the vendor and the programme team: the vendor clearly understood what Spire as their client considered important at any given 'now' moment so that focus could be given to those issues, and the programme team were forced to prioritize their issues across multiple projects and articulate them clearly.

This process was so successful that the vendor has now adopted the Exceed process for internal use, and is now following the same process to measure, monitor and score customer satisfaction.

STEP 7: LAUNCH THE EXCEED PROCESS

'Remember that the success of your project will ultimately be measured by whether your sponsor and stakeholders feel they got the benefits they wanted in a way they expected,' writes Susanne Madsen in her book, *The Project Management Coaching Workbook* (2011: 174). 'To avoid the perception of failure, not only do you need to clearly define the objective success criteria ... you also need to turn any subjective and qualitative feelings and statements into quantitative and measurable conditions.'

In April 2010, we set out to do this and launched Exceed with this programme by carrying out the survey at one hospital. In practice, we carried out this step at the same time as we were talking to vendors (Step 6). Using the approach that had worked so successfully in service delivery, we recorded the results on a spreadsheet. Shenhar et al. (2002) demonstrated that documentation is the most powerful way of communicating with project stakeholders, so we wanted to ensure that the results were captured and shared appropriately.

This first review coincided with a system-wide outage, and the discussion and scores reflected that. Even so, the overall result for that business unit was 6.75 (Good).

STEP 8: DELIVER ON THE ISSUES

The results from that Exceed discussion did flag up some interesting things that the project team was able to quickly do something about. For example, there was an issue with the vendor service that we had not previously identified. This was passed to the vendor to resolve. There was also a concern that not enough training had been carried out, so the team looked at ways to address this. The opportunity to flag up issues outside regular team meetings meant that we engaged in more dialogue with project customers. It also ensured that the project managers working on this programme had a better understanding of the issues that were being faced by hospital staff, and they could build this learning into future plans.

A further advantage – although one we can only prove anecdotally – is that by taking a customer-centric view, and having project managers on site with their customers really taking an interest in the customer's environment and challenges, led to more understanding and support from customers when times were difficult. All large programmes have their share of ups and downs, and this one was no different. However, it felt as if customers were more forgiving as they understood that the team was trying to do its best by them.

The results over time also showed something surprising: even though the verbatim comments were 90 per cent constructive criticism, when asked to put a number to the level of service the project team provided, the numbers were consistently higher than the comments would lead us to expect. We would see this pattern over the following months in other hospitals and it led us to conclude that clinical staff were more generous with their scores than their administrative or executive colleagues!

AFTER THE PROGRAMME

The programme finished at the beginning of 2011. During this time, other projects had also started to use the Exceed spreadsheet and process to gather feedback from customers and this continued when the radiology programme ended. These projects used the same categories of managing project issues, communication, and overall perception, but replaced the question about integrating project deliverables with one focused on how well the project was being managed to the customer's timeframe. This was as a result of the PMO recognizing that projects were often delivering later than expected owing to unforeseen issues and we wanted to uncover whether time to delivery was really a concern for our project customers. It turned out that in most cases it wasn't.

We also made a small change in the way in which scores were gathered. Some of the IT projects were so small, and had such engaged customers who fully understood the purpose and value of the Exceed process, that we let these project customers respond in writing. The Exceed template was emailed to them, they added both their scores and verbatim comments, and returned the template to the project manager. This was often a faster way of getting feedback from a community of healthcare practitioners who were not always able to focus on IT project work during the hours that the project manager was available. We also felt that project customers may be more inclined to be more honest if they were one step removed from the project manager through email, and thus expected the results to be lower. This approach contradicts the research findings of Klakegg et al., who conclude that one of the most powerful practices in interviewing project stakeholders about potential issues is to discuss the situation with those involved. This allows for assumptions to be 'explored, challenged, and discussed, rather than presenting them only as a final or closed written statement' (2010: 148).

With hindsight, Klakegg and his colleagues were right. We do believe you get a richer and more useful picture from oral conversations with project customers instead of through written transcripts, although we noticed no difference in scores between those reviews carried out in person or over the phone and those done via email.

One of the challenges of gathering tangible evidence of customer satisfaction is having to prioritize the responses. As we saw, many of the issues raised to service delivery related to several themes, and by addressing these, many of the 180 concerns raised were quickly addressed. Project customers on one project often do not have the same issues as customers on another project. Individual project managers liaised with each other and with colleagues in other teams to address the issues raised. We never had a prioritization problem, but this could be a challenge for other teams using the Exceed process. The most valuable part of this collaboration from the customer's perspective is the feedback on the issue that they raised, specifically the project manager returning to the customer with clarification about the problem, or better yet, a resolution.

The overall results between April 2010 and October 2011, averaged across the four survey dimensions, are shown in the Figure 6.1.

INTERPRETING THE RESULTS

The results in Figure 6.1 show a good story, but not the sharp increase in scores that were shown in service delivery. Interpreting the results from the project environment uncovers five points.

1. Each month the consolidated Exceed score relates to one, two or three projects only, not every project in the portfolio.
2. Since the radiology programme ended, the learning from each project does not overlap so meaningfully with other projects.
3. As not every project is surveyed every month, the reviews are not carried out by the same person every month. The results could differ based on the fact that a different project manager is asking a different group of stakeholders and they have a different interpretation of Good, Very Good and Excellent.
4. Verbatim comments did not always appear to match the scores given. In one review in June 2010, communication was flagged as not being as good as it could be, and the customer provided the project manager with a specific example of poor communication. However, the score for this element was still 9 out of 10 (Consistently Very Good).
5. The reviews often uncovered issues that were not to do with the projects at all, such as system downtime and issues with suppliers.

The project management team has attempted to manage these points.

Not Surveying Every Project

The project lifecycle may only be long enough for the project to go through an Exceed review once. As a result, the scores do not reliably show progression in performance across all the projects, and a particularly difficult (or good) project or month can skew the results. The flip side to this is that the flexibility of the metrics means that the projects can be measured individually over time, or that scores from several projects can be aggregated or averaged. There is also the risk that the Exceed spreadsheet is seen as an alternative type of post-implementation review, instead of continuous mechanism for gathering feedback and managing customer expectations.

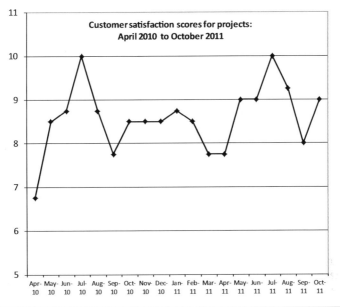

	Average	Issues	Communication	Integration	Overall progress
2010					
April	6.75	7	5	8	7
May	8.5	10	8	8	8
June	8.75	9	9	8	9
July	10	10	10	10	10
August	8.75	9	9	8	9
September	7.75	6	10	8	7
October	8.5	10	9	7	8
November	8.5	9	9	8	8
December	8.5	10	9	6	9
2011					
January	8.75	9	9	9	8
February	8.5	8	8	9	9
March	7.75	5	9	7	10
April	7.75	5	9	7	10
May	9	9	9	9	9
June	9	9	9	9	9
July	10	10	10	10	10
August	9.25	9	10	8	10
September	8	8	8	8	8
October	9	9	9	9	9

Figure 6.1   Customer satisfaction scores for projects at Spire Healthcare between April 2010 and October 2011

The learning here is that Exceed reviews have to start early enough in the project lifecycle to enable the project manager to do something about the issues flagged. Projects with a short lifecycle may only have one Exceed review, but this should be timed to be held at a significant moment in the project, normally after the major deliverable has been completed but before project closure. The project manager also maintains a customer-centric outlook regardless of how many Exceed reviews fit within the project lifecycle. This means that however short the project, they are still able to consistently monitor progress and keep the project customers informed at every step, which are two things that Papke-Shields et al. (2010) have shown to increase the chance of project success.

Sharing Learning Between Projects

There are still some points raised by customers about process that can be shared effectively and improved in order to make an impact on all stakeholder of projects in the portfolio. Having said that, we felt this challenge was not as important to address in the early days. Where process changes improved all future projects, that was an advantage, but as long as individual project customers felt they were getting an improved service from the project managers and team, that was considered more important. We wanted to see increases in levels of engagement and collaboration with project customers before turning our attention to long term improvements. With hindsight, we could have done both at the same time.

Inconsistent Month-on-month Results

This was a significant learning point for the project teams and the PMO team. It is possible to explain statistical blips by virtue of the fact that different project managers were asking and different stakeholders were responding to the Exceed questions. Aggregating the results provides a high-level picture which is adequate for the purposes of the PMO but does require context to be fully understood.

We realized that ideally the same stakeholders should be targeted regularly as the social capital, trust and engagement that this builds up along the way is useful in a crisis. Project teams need excellent relationships with key stakeholders, as we saw in Chapter 2, and not talking to them regularly about their customer experiences on the project meant missing out on valuable information.

Verbatim Comments not Matching Scores

When the project is going well and the customers are satisfied, they don't want to give bad scores. People are generally reasonable, especially when the conversation hinges on what the project manager can do for them or should be doing differently to help them meet their needs. We decided to take no action about this point and just enjoy human nature!

Non-project Issues Raised

How many times have you complained to someone (maybe a customer service agent in a call centre) about a problem that you know they cannot resolve? Project customers are no different, and they took the opportunity to raise issues that were unrelated to the project but were broadly to do with IT or third-party suppliers. Any issues raised as part of the discussions that were not project-related were passed on to the correct team to deal with.

The five points above demonstrate the PMO and team focus on customer-centric project management. As well as this, all project managers continue to have personal objectives set that relate to the successful completion of Exceed reviews for their projects. This has contributed to the mindset shift in delivering good customer service to project customers instead of simply delivering to the triple constraint.

There is much to consider when looking at the graph of results but the overarching point is that the graph itself doesn't really matter. The metrics hold the project managers accountable, but the graph isn't the story. The story is in how the project managers embraced – individually and as a team – a customer-centric mindset that shifted feedback from customers from responses like, 'Needed more support' and 'Didn't understand the impact of the project' in April 2010 to, 'The project manager has worked incredibly hard throughout the whole project and her involvement has been very much appreciated by myself and my team,' in October 2011. Two of the project managers have won internal company awards for going above and beyond the day job in the service of the project customers.

Metrics are useless unless someone acts on them, so the real achievement is not that we started using a new spreadsheet and publishing the satisfaction levels every month, but that we orchestrated a mindset shift to dealing with the issues that were raised as a result of our customer-centric meetings with project stakeholders.

The metrics provide the opportunity for Spire's project managers to be excellent despite the challenges of a complex organization, and for customers to feel fully engaged in the project management lifecycle.

KEY POINTS:

- A reliance on post-implementation reviews restricts proactivity.
- Tailor engagement methods to suit needs of customers: use email or have conversations over the phone if it helps you get the data you require.
- The process can also highlight surprisingly happy customers.
- Satisfied customers make useful allies in difficult times.

CHAPTER 7

REFINING YOUR CUSTOMER-CENTRIC APPROACH

During 2011, Spire Healthcare embarked on another ambitious IT project, to install a new back-end financial processing system. The first six months of this initiative were a difficult journey. The project was highly collaborative, involving a number of third parties and representatives from all areas of the Spire business, both administrative and support functions and patient-facing staff in hospitals. A dedicated cross-functional team was put together to run this project, scattered across the UK and Europe. Business as usual work and other projects had to continue during this time. Exceed was still in use on these other projects but was not used during the early days of the finance system project.

After almost exactly six months, the core project team was struggling with low morale. The lead project manager was on the verge of resigning. A key project stakeholder was unhappy with the performance of the IT team, resulting in a change of personnel. A major system issue was uncovered which changed the development and deployment strategy, leading the steering group to question the project's direction. Many staff felt overworked trying to keep up with the constant changes in a dynamic environment while working in what felt like a vacuum of information. These concerns, evident in the 'lived experience' of the project, are the early warning signs of an initiative in trouble (Klakegg et al. 2010).

Together, the team addressed these issues, starting with the vacuum of information. They produced a regular project newsletter. The frequency of status meetings was increased and the number of people attending rose: contrary to what you might think, this made the team more productive.

Given the scale of the project, many of the core customers were almost working full-time on the project. They would be the recipients of the deliverables eventually, but for now were seconded to the project. Applying the principles of customer-centric project management to people on the project team was another mindset change for the project manager. However, knowing how important it was to ensure that all customer groups felt truly engaged with this initiative, the Exceed process was started as the visible output of the customer-centric project management approach.

MANAGING MULTIPLE STAKEHOLDER GROUPS

Up until this point, Exceed had only been used for projects and programmes with discrete groups of stakeholders and one key beneficiary. The finance system project touched many groups of stakeholders. Whom would we ask on this project? We could ask the finance team, but that would exclude valuable input from the hospital-based staff. We could ask the hospital administrators, but this would mean overlooking the views of the head office finance community, who were essential to the successful delivery of the project. We could ask the project sponsor, but leading this project was 80 per cent of his day job and we spoke to him daily anyway. He was heavily involved in the project management processes and decisions, so we already felt closer to his views than those of any other stakeholder. We also had third parties involved, and were completing work packages to hand over to them. They were also project customers. In the end, the project manager decided to ask them all.

This was a change to the way that the PMO had used Exceed in the past for other projects. The other main change made to the standard Exceed process was allowing project customers to choose their own questions. Service delivery had done this when Exceed was launched, but the PMO had previously determined the questions on behalf of the customers. As Dvir et al. (1998) show, what defines success for one stakeholder or project is not always the same for another. 'Comprehensive success criteria must therefore reflect different interests and views which leads to the necessity for a multidimensional, multicriteria approach,' they write.

Given the number of customer groups, we took this approach, and prepared to deal with a complex matrix of multiple success criteria. As each new stakeholder was targeted, the project manager asked him or her to explain what they felt was most important. These 'top of mind' concerns were then translated to questions. The anticipation was that each project customer would have their own set of tailored, meaningful questions, reflecting the fact that the project's successes and challenges would be different for each of them. As Shenhar and Dvir (2007) comment, success criteria can change over the life of a project, and we wanted to create a model that would enable stakeholders to change what was important to them as the project progressed. In practice, there were several general themes that made constructing a spreadsheet to record the feedback easier than we had initially thought.

When the project customers were asked what they considered most important, and what as a project team we should be focusing on to deliver to the best possible outcomes to meet their objectives, communication and planning were the most frequent responses. We adopted the headings of Communication and Proactivity to cover these areas and bundled all the other questions under the heading of Quality of Project Delivery. This covered things like decision-making, resource planning and a multitude of other topics that different stakeholder groups considered important.

In this way, each individual project customer could have a targeted, individual, satisfaction survey just for them, but we could still consolidate the results at a project level to provide an overall picture of satisfaction with the project and the deliverables.

Appendix 3 shows the template used to gather customer satisfaction scores for this project. The focus on the top three project issues, as seen by the customer, and the increase in number of topics make for a deeper conversation about project success criteria and enable these to be tailored per customer. The table below shows how the feedback from different customer groups is consolidated at a project level to provide an overall picture on a monthly basis. The customer groups represented are two internal departments who are recipients of the project deliverables, the IT team and a third-party implementation partner.

Table 7.1   Summary customer satisfaction for Project X, January 2012

Exceed customer satisfaction record: Project X		

Average customer satisfaction	Acceptable	5.33

Summary of key stakeholder satisfaction		
Average service rating: business areas	Good	6.00
Average service rating: IT	Very Poor	2.00
Average service rating: implementation partners	Very Good	8.00

Supporting individual measures					
Stakeholders	Top 3 issues	Communication	Proactivity	Project quality	Average
Business area 1	5	6	5	6	5.50
Business area 2	6	7	6	7	6.50
IT (internal customer)	2	2	2	2	2.00
Implementation partner	8	8	8	8	8.00
Average service rating	5.25	5.75	5.25	5.75	5.50

INTERPRETING THE NEW EXCEED SCORES

Offering customers the opportunity to select their own top measures (even though these were then grouped under the headings above) produced some interesting results. The team fully expected one of the implementation partners to say that timely payment was a key success factor for them: after all, they were providing a service and needed to be paid for it. This commercial aspect of the project did not rate highly with them at all – it was seen as a hygiene factor, just something that would happen automatically in the background. What did concern them, and what subsequently became their success criteria, was facilitating communication between workstreams and ensuring documentation was approved in a timely manner. This enabled the project team, working collaboratively with the implementation partner, to develop ways to ensure that communication was happening appropriately and as soon as practical across the distributed team.

The team also discovered that colleagues from the same department – other people working in IT – scored the project most harshly. This highlighted the fact that much of the project team's efforts had been in communicating out to other departments and working on engaging project customers, at the expense of people a few desks away. The poor scores could also be seen as a consequence of being more critical of our own failings: knowing what the ideal project management processes should be, it was perhaps easier to identify where our methods – however good they appeared to the customer – fell short of the gold standard.

What has been abundantly clear throughout the process of using Exceed with multiple stakeholder groups is the fact that different individuals have different priorities. One project customer considered resource planning a priority, but reporting was important to another and the testing approach important to a third. The experience of using tailored questions per customer highlights the inherent weakness in the original Exceed template: asking everyone the same set of questions may make tracking at a PMO level easier, but it does not genuinely reflect what is important to any one stakeholder at any one time. The project team is expecting these measures of success to change as the project progresses, so the summary headings may no longer be appropriate as the project moves into the later stages. The benefit of this model is that it takes no time at all to amend a spreadsheet or table, and any changes can easily be incorporated to ensure that the customer satisfaction measures stay up to date and relevant.

Our experience of using this process to manage feedback from multiple customer groups still has a way to go, as it is a relatively new tweak to our customer-centric approach. At the time of writing, the project is still in progress and we only have a few months' worth of data for this 'tailored' Exceed. It remains to be seen whether this approach is categorically successful, although the early results are very positive. Further research comparing the levels of engagement and reported project success metrics between 'standard' Exceed with the 'tailored' Exceed is something that could be undertaken in the future.

FINDING TIME TO FIX THE PROBLEMS

Identifying the issues through the Exceed process is a start, but customer-centric project management is about more than just numbers in a table. The purpose of measuring customer satisfaction is to be able to actively do something about the issues raised as part of the discussion with the project customer.

This is relatively easy with one project customer, but using the tailored model and talking to customers with different priorities makes the project team's life more complicated. They are expected to deliver solutions to the issues raised, and doing so for four customers is more work than doing so for one. The project still needs to be managed, and day jobs have to be done.

Project managers globally have to do more with less to be able to respond appropriately to the challenges of the new business paradigm identified in Chapter 3. Finding the time to respond to issues raised as part of Exceed is a key part of the customer-centric mindset, but this has to be balanced with other project responsibilities and potentially, for team members not working full-time on the project, their operational duties as well. By now, you know that we think customers count. There is always time to do right by your customers, even if doing right at that particular moment means explaining why you cannot tackle the issue they raised until a release has been shipped or the next big milestone has been reached. Issues have to be prioritized and sometimes cannot be dealt with during that month. If the topic is still raised at the next discussion, it is clear to the customer and the project manager that not enough energy has been put into resolving this problem, or at least improving it. Customers will be quick to show this in the scores.

This level of transparency and focus provides a better quality result for the project overall, better customer engagement and all round better morale in the wider project team. Customer-centric project management revolves around being able to deliver to promises, and the Exceed model is the tool that enables customers to hold project managers accountable for resolving issues.

EXCEED IN LARGE PROJECTS

The Exceed process can be tailored easily, which means it can be adapted for use in large or complex projects where there are multiple stakeholder groups. The same implementation approach can be used, but you will need to adapt Step 3 (Identify the customer) to allow for the fact that the project has multiple customer groups. You will also need to establish how you want to engage with these groups. Depending on the project, one set of questions could be appropriate for all of them, or like the case study example above, you may decide that different questions for different customers is the best way to go. You could even let customers prioritize their own key focus areas and generate questions from those. This will let you really get to the bottom of what success looks like for each individual.

The metrics for multi-customer group projects are administered in exactly the same way, with the exception that you will need a method to roll up the scores into one consolidated score per reporting period. With different questions per customer, this could be difficult, so it is worth putting together a spreadsheet where the results can be recorded. Appendix 3 will give you a starting point.

EXCEED IN HEALTHCARE AND OTHER INDUSTRIES

This chapter and the previous two chapters have focused on customer centricity in a healthcare environment in both IT service delivery and IT project teams. There are a lot of challenges for projects in healthcare. Technology is expensive and changes quickly; by the time the radiology programme described in Chapter 6 was into its third year there was already new technology on the market and the programme team had to adapt in order to incorporate and retrofit advances to the system. Clinical and administrative staff in hospitals often work shifts, which means they are not always available for project meetings or to attend training when required. When hospital staff are on shift, their priority is providing excellent customer service to patients and their clinical colleagues, not attending IT project meetings. On several occasions project team meetings have been interrupted by nurses or theatre staff having to leave the room to attend to patients. This is how it should be, and IT is a service that fits around their needs, not the other way round. Customer-centric project management has enabled project managers to refocus their efforts on what adds value to the project customer, which in many cases is a longer, more flexible implementation timescale that fits around the operational requirements of working in a hospital.

IT is an industry that works in a highly collaborative way (Herzog 2001) and it may be that Exceed as a tool to drive customer centricity is more successful with IT projects because of the context of partnership that often exists between project team and third-party vendor. Different industries and verticals have different challenges. However, we believe that the process and approach explained here is adaptable enough for you to make it work in your industry, with your project customers. Your project managers can also become customer-centric and build a working, positive partnership with their colleagues outside the PMO. Chapter 8 explains how you can make this work in your organization.

KEY POINTS:

- Customer-centric project management is a mindset that includes everyone. This can be reflected by modifying the Exceed process to include a full cross-section of business customers.
- Different groups value different things. Use specific measures for each group.
- Make sure your own house is in order. Don't forget support groups and implementation teams in your own department who you may not usually consider as project customers.
- Customer-centric project management is for all projects, but you can tailor the process to each specific project.

CHAPTER 8

IMPLEMENTING EXCEED

As we saw in Chapter 5, there are eight simple steps involved in implementing the Exceed process. In Chapters 6 and 7 we saw how these steps had been put into practice in a project environment at Spire Healthcare, our case study organization. Once you have decided that you want to reap the benefits of customer-centric project management the next step is to implement the Exceed process in your organization. In this chapter we will look at those eight steps again and provide a generic deployment plan for implementing Exceed in any organization. This focuses on implementation in a project environment, but as you have seen from the service delivery examples provided for healthcare and financial services, Exceed can also be used in other departments. Adapt the framework below for your use so that it is most appropriate for your organization.

Depending on the size and complexity of the organization, the process can be established in its entirety in any timeframe between a single day or a few weeks.

STEP 1: SUPPORT FOR THE VISION: OBTAIN BUY IN FROM THE ULTIMATE AUTHORITY

The most senior business leader or executive must believe wholeheartedly in the concept of customer centricity and drive his or her organization with a single-minded determination to achieve the vision: 'Every customer of company/department/project team XYZ will continually rate the services we provide as Good, Very Good or Excellent.' From the time of launch, your customer-centric culture change and the tools you use to support it require the highest level of sponsorship, like any business critical initiative.

In a project environment this role is likely to be filled by the PMO director, or the board member responsible for project portfolios. In an organization with a functional hierarchy, each division may have its own project managers and the director responsible for each division may take the role of sponsoring the Exceed process in their area.

In our experience, gaining buy in for customer centricity is not difficult to achieve. In fact, it is hard to imagine any senior PMO leader who would not be interested in knowing how customers rate their division. The Exceed process delivers very rapid results so there is no need to set long-term targets for improvement, which means staff members are not tied up implementing a new process when they should be delivering projects. Having said this, timescales need to be realistic and appropriate for the organization.

While the overall vision should be kept firmly in mind there is real value in setting interim targets. Example targets could be:

- Three weeks from now, we will have baselined performance on all projects by completing one Exceed review per project.
- Three months from now, half of our project customers will have measured us as 'Good'.
- Six months from now, less than 10 per cent of our project customers will view us as Poor.

STEP 2: EDUCATE THE ORGANIZATION: SPREAD THE VISION

Thomas and Mullaly (2008) show that when companies stop trying to improve project management approaches, organizations stop seeing benefit from project management techniques. This is a strong argument for continuous process improvement in the PMO, and implementing customer-centric project management techniques is one way to continue to build on past successes with project processes, or to inject a straightforward process to a new PMO to see some quick returns on that investment.

However, in order to make customer centricity a success, you have to spread the word about the new focus on customers. Every member of the project management division or PMO will need to understand that they have embarked on a process which is important, not only to their particular project, but to themselves and the business they support. This can be adopted into the existing PMO culture of continuous improvement. In fact, every action, every decision, every process, every project will be considered from a single viewpoint – how does this affect our customers? Questions like the following need to be discussed at a PMO or programme level:

- Will this process or action benefit project customers?
- Would they agree?
- How will we know what they think of this?
- Will it help them achieve their objectives?
- Will this process adversely affect our relationship with our customers?

When project managers are asking these kinds of questions, they are already thinking in a customer-centric way. This kind of thinking should not require a major shift in direction. Each role in the PMO, from portfolio manager to project co-ordinator, exists to serve customers and every action must be geared towards creating a best possible result in the eyes of the customer. Every individual's actions affect the customer experience in some shape or form.

STEP 3: DECIDE WHO THE CUSTOMER IS

Exceed seeks to address the three most critical questions of any quality-oriented process from day one:

1. Who are our customers?
2. What do they want?
3. And how do we know they are getting it?

In order to answer the first question, the PMO must organize the Exceed process in a way which is relevant to the significance of each component part of the business. For example, if the PMO is aligned on a functional basis, with teams of project managers facing off to different functional areas like sales, manufacturing or logistics, this could involve separate measurement of service to these functions. All sales projects would use the same questions and measures, and logistics projects would use a separate set of measures. These could be broken down even further if necessary. In car manufacturing, for example, Exceed measures could apply separately to engine build, test, paint shop, axle build, body in white, despatch, marketing, dealerships and so on. For some businesses such as those who deliver professional service projects, the most relevant groupings could be by external customer: Customer A rates us as Good for project delivery, Customer B rates us as poor, and so on.

STEP 4: DEFINE A SIMPLE SCORING MECHANISM WHICH CUSTOMERS CAN USE TO RATE THE SERVICES THEY RECEIVE

Most customers can relate to the simple idea of a satisfaction rating of between 1 and 10. If your project managers and project customers are used to working with Red/Amber/Green (RAG) statuses, you can colour code the ratings:

- 1 to 4 is Red;
- 5 is Amber;
- 6 and above is Green.

Alternatively, develop a scale that makes sense to you and aligns with your existing metrics.

STEP 5: ORGANIZE FOR SUCCESS

It is vital to establish a function within the PMO tasked with meeting the customer (in person or virtually) in order to understand their needs on an ongoing basis. Let's call this Customer Services for the sake of a name. The PMO team will need to decide how best to resource this role. Options are:

1. Appoint one person to do all the Exceed reviews for all projects. This could be a full-time or part-time responsibility depending on the size of the organization.
2. Split the role between a number of existing PMO functions so that the requirement to carry out reviews is not on one person.
3. Require each project manager to take responsibility for reviews on their own projects, with central administrative support for collating results.

You may be able to think of an alternative way to resource this function.

There are some advantages to having this Customer Services function as a discrete PMO role not carried out by the project manager. Feedback is more likely to be impartial and the interpretation of the results could be more standardized. The disadvantage is that the person in that role then has to meet the project manager to feed back the remarks provided and handover any issues that need resolving.

Our recommendation is option three, with the project manager taking responsibility for carrying out reviews on their own projects. This avoids the risk that customers lack clarity on whether to follow up their remarks to the Exceed reviewer or their project manager. If the project manager, who has knowledge of the context of the project, is present at the review then he or she may be able to resolve some issues on the spot. It also ensures that the focus on customer centricity is not 'someone else's problem' and encourages project managers to work in this way on a long-term basis.

It is also essential that the people carrying out this function are equipped to do so. It is preferable to have individuals who understand how the business works and who possess the appropriate behaviours for the role. These people would have advanced listening and communication skills, empathy and attention to detail, backed by detailed knowledge of the workings of the company, particularly in relation to how projects work and how the PMO functions.

This customer services role is not normally part of the job description for a project manager. If project managers are to take on this responsibility as part of their normal project duties, there may have to be an education intervention to ensure that they understand both the rationale behind this move and that they have the skills required to fulfil it. In short, this new breed of customer-centric project managers is critical to providing a more customer-friendly and efficient single reference point for project customers. It is now their business to own every customer issue from the moment it is raised to the moment it is resolved.

In this regard the customer services element of their role could be seen to be purely reactive but, in practice, this is not the case. As the Exceed process develops, the emphasis moves to proactive engagement as the customer-centric project manager seeks out potential issues and provides early communication for project milestones. Some sample text for inclusion in job descriptions, or as the basis for a dedicated customer services role, is available in Appendix 4.

The project prioritization process can also be reconsidered in the light of customer centricity, although you may want to wait until it is fully embedded before organizing this process around the Exceed process. Once the organization has fully adopted a customer-centric mindset, the Exceed process will assist with prioritization. Certain projects will struggle to answer the question, 'How does this help us to be rated as 'Good, Very Good or Excellent' by our customers/consumers?' Project business cases that fail to show how the company's consumers will benefit from the project could be prioritized lower than those that do. Including Exceed targets or measures in project business cases could be done as a matter of routine. While project business cases will most likely always emphasize financial measures, Exceed provides a supplementary way to rank projects in a portfolio.

It is not just project managers and the PMO that needs to organize for success. For the rest of the business there is much more to do than talk to project customers. The success of a customer-centric approach depends totally on the ability of the business to respond immediately and positively to the customer issues. Issues must be resolved to the customer's satisfaction – this is the only way that scores improve and that project teams can be said to be truly providing value to their customers. Project managers should have the support of their colleagues in other divisions to ensure that issues relating to customer service and perception are given priority. This is likely to be, in the first instance, their project teams, and project managers can manage these resources to respond quickly to problems. However, it may also include sharing the Exceed implementation plans with third-party vendors or colleagues in other areas of the business and ensuring that they are also on board with the vision and how it is to be achieved, so that they can also align their efforts to support the successful resolution of project issues.

This may sound daunting, and it may involve a certain amount of reappraisal of some departmental activities but there should be no need for major cultural improvement initiatives to ensure that customer satisfaction is at the forefront of people's minds. It is merely a matter of focus.

STEP 6: ALIGN BUSINESS PARTNERS WITH EXCEED: BRING THEM INTO THE PROCESS

Project managers fully bought into the concepts of customer-centric project management can reasonably point to the fact that much of what they deliver is outsourced or provided through contracted suppliers. Their ability to directly influence every activity and process is, therefore, limited: however good you are, the service you provide project customers is only as good as the weakest link. Don't let suppliers and outsourcing partners undermine your efforts at delivering excellent service. Extend the customer-centric mindset and the Exceed process to your third-party partners.

There are two ways to engage suppliers in this process: acting as a customer of their services and treating them as a customer of your services.

a) Acting as a customer. Exceed can be used effectively to rate the performance of suppliers or external service providers. Suppliers often suffer as a result of the lack of meaningful metrics against which they can perform and Exceed solves this problem. Project managers, while they serve their project customers, are also customers themselves. Acting as the customer of the third party, they can agree an individual set of Exceed measures with the vendor during contract negotiations for the project. This can be particularly valuable in software projects where continued engagement with the vendor is essential for the success of the project, and where the relationships with the vendor will pass into the operational environment. Choose measures that focus on aspects of the relationship that are wider than merely performance against a service agreement or contractual metrics. In this way, suppliers receive more insight and clarity into what really matters to their project customers and as such have a much improved chance of securing a successful and enduring relationship with the project team, and the operational team after project closure. This can also significantly reduce the level of risk inherent in projects when partners are involved.

Convincing a supplier to adopt a customer-centric mindset is perhaps more difficult than launching Exceed as an internal process. Explaining what is in it for the supplier is essential for gaining buy-in. As well as better levels of engagement with the project team and lower risk, which should in turn make the relationship more profitable for them, you could also implement incentives. We have implemented Exceed programmes where outsourcers qualified for monthly financial bonuses directly linked to the attainment of satisfaction ratings provided by project stakeholders.

b) Treating them as a customer. Suppliers want the project to be successful, just as a business customer wants it to be successful. Project managers responsible for managing the ongoing relationship with a vendor during the lifecycle of the project can approach them as they would any other project customer, by asking about their top issues and how they can be of help during this project phase. Partners will have particular issues which need to be managed. Some might even relate to elements outside project delivery, such as late payment of bills.

In short, customer-centric project management requires suppliers to be treated as equals. Approaches such as procurement performance reviews as set out by the *PMBOK® Guide* (2008) are typically a one-way discussion on project status. Using Exceed can make these discussions more targeted and valuable to both the supplier and the project team.

In our experience, outsourcing partners have fully embraced this approach. Most have seized the opportunity to demonstrate their wider capabilities and have been extremely enthusiastic to join in the process, despite the risks and challenges of the outsourcing relationship identified in Chapter 3. The ongoing dialogue provides clarity that they have not previously had, as Exceed involves both sides agreeing the necessary measures around deliverables, behaviours, attitudes, levels of proactivity, flexibility and anything else that constitutes an excellent working relationship for this project.

For example, we worked with a technical supplier whose service was poor. The management team was disinterested and lethargic. The first set of Exceed scores provided to them by the project manager for this project was a wakeup call: no measurement area scored above 3 out of 10 (Consistently Poor). The management team committed to the Exceed vision. They wanted to be scored as Good, Very Good or Excellent by their project customers.

We were honest about their performance, and they were honest about the challenges they faced with improving the scores. It was a large organization; changing working practices was going to be a slow job. We agreed to split the Exceed measures into two dimensions, relationship and service, to better reflect their efforts and what we collectively were trying to achieve. Within three months, relationship scores had soared past Good. After six months both relationship and service dimensions scored 9 (Consistently Very Good). Once they knew what was important to their customers, they were able to address it, leading to a better project result, and a more profitable relationship all round.

STEP 7: LAUNCH THE EXCEED PROCESS

The first face-to-face customer meeting is held in order to explain how the process operates. Some Exceed meetings are attended by heads of divisions or departments, but normally the project sponsor or their delegated representative is present. It should be someone (or more than one person) who has a detailed knowledge of the working of the project, and it does not need to be someone senior or with a lot of power in the organizational hierarchy.

The first meeting typically goes like this. The project manager or whoever has responsibility for the process introduces themselves as that customer's prime point of contact with full authority and accountability for resolution and feedback of issues 24 hours a day, 7 days a week, 365 days a year. While this may seem a strange first point for the agenda, it is possible that the project customer has never met the project manager previously, or never thought of the project manager or PMO as providing this type of service.

The project manager then explains the simple customer-centric vision ('Every customer will rate our services as Good, Very Good or Excellent') and emphasizes that full support for the Exceed process has been given from the head of the business unit right through the entire organization and that the process will continue throughout the life of the project. They could also share some results from other projects that have gone through the process, highlighting issues that were resolved or process improvements that were made as a result of the Exceed interventions, and demonstrating the practical output of customer centricity.

Together, the meeting attendees establish the ongoing frequency of the Exceed meetings and agree who should attend. Attendees and format are completely fluid and open to change at any point. Monthly meetings seem most appropriate in order to give the project manager a chance to produce an effective response but again, this frequency is at the discretion of the customer. Early resolutions are of course communicated immediately.

The project manager agrees the areas of service or deliverables against which performance can be scored or rated. Some customers struggle with this idea, chiefly because no one has ever asked them the question. In cases like this generic questions can be suggested such as:

1. How well do we manage your project issues?
2. How well do we communicate with you?
3. How proactive are we?
4. How would you rate the service quality you receive from us?

These questions work well for the purposes of producing an Exceed template to structure future discussions. It is perfectly legitimate for the PMO or project manager to suggest areas of measurement but the customer's measures are the most important ones, for all the reasons we saw in Chapter 2. If a project customer defines that the most important measure to them is the production of the ABCXYZ report in triplicate no later than 2.38 p.m. on a Thursday afternoon, then that measure will be recorded accordingly.

We strongly recommend that the first question above ('How well do we manage your project issues?') is agreed with the customer as an Exceed measure. Project issues are often prioritized using high/medium/low categories and those issues categorized as low may take a long time to resolve. Without asking, you will never know if this is the most pressing concern for the customer at that moment in time.

To provide a real-life example of this, during one project team meeting the point that there was no data migration strategy for the project was raised by the customer. The project team did not consider this to be a problem at all: this was a project with a long lifecycle and the data migration work was easily a year away. The work to scope out the data migration strategy was on the project plan and scheduled to start in a couple of months. It was a non-issue as far as the project team were concerned. However, the project customer continued to press the point in the next meeting. The project team refocused their efforts and spent a short time preparing a high level document explaining the next steps for the data migration activities. This was to be fleshed out in a more detailed work package later in the project, but it provided the assurance that the project customer needed that this critical element had not been overlooked and was being dealt with professionally and early. Feeling more reassured about this element of the project, the project customer was able to concentrate on and contribute to other elements of the project.

The way in which the project manager responds to the resolution of the customer's top project issues is instrumental in turning around poor customer satisfaction and ensuring that the project provides both actual value and the perception of value. The time taken to resolve the customer's top project issues gives an immediate indicator of the project team's commitment and corresponds directly to the speed that customer satisfaction ratings will rise.

The 'top project issues' list is a simple idea, but few PMOs can pull out a list of the most pressing issues felt by their customers on any given day. Customer-centric organizations running Exceed in a project environment can not only do this across a portfolio of projects, but can demonstrate who is tasked with resolution and when that resolution has been agreed with the customer. It is, however, essential to limit the discussion of top project issues to only three. The project manager should explain that, while all issues will be recorded, only the top three will be prioritized for action unless exceptional circumstances are involved. Issue resolution must be paired with continued project delivery, not just for this project but for all projects in the portfolio, and there is only so much that the PMO and project managers can take on and continue to do a good job. The good news is that the top three issues should trip off the customer's tongue and are most likely to relate to here and now situations.

Once the metrics have been agreed and scored at the first meeting, these can be recorded centrally so that metrics across the portfolio of projects can be gathered. Do be careful when recording and publishing the results of review meetings. Some reviews may include discussions about individuals, and watch out for any personal information captured, especially if the individual is being used in an example of where things are not going so well. Provide feedback to the individual concerned in a constructive way and consider editing personal information from any data published publicly.

STEP 8: DELIVER ON THE ISSUES

Improvements in customer relationships and scores only come from being able to deal with issues. If a rapid resolution can be provided to these issues you should see a major improvement in customer satisfaction and the implications this has for collaborative working and project progress. Once these resolutions have been fed back and resolved there will be space to agree the new top three issues at the next meeting.

Some issues will take longer than a month to resolve, and may come up time and time again. Stick with it, and deliver improvements incrementally if that helps tackle them. The kudos and credibility that comes from making improvements to the situation will be worth it, and will demonstrate unequivocally to customers that you really are customer-centric.

Project managers will initially face a daunting list of issues, especially if they are managing several projects concurrently. Past experience has proved that centralized management of this top issues list provides the most efficient way to track these issues through to resolution and feedback. The PMO can provide this function.

The eight steps to implementing the Exceed process and the associated actions are summarized in Table 8.1.

Table 8.1   Exceed implementation guide

Step	Description	Actions	Responsibility
1	Support for the vision: obtain buy in from the ultimate authority	• Prepare justification for customer-centric project management approach • Arrange meeting with PMO leader	PMO, C-suite executives
2	Educate the organization: spread the vision	• Arrange and hold briefing meetings to introduce customer-centric project management and Exceed process to a wider audience	PMO
3	Decide who the customer is	• Decide if process will focus on one customer per project or several • Agree roles that form the project customer base, allowing for the fact this could be different between projects	PMO and project managers
4	Define a simple scoring mechanism which customers can use to rate the services they receive	• Produce rating scale • Gain agreement on scale	PMO
5	Organize for success	• Prepare customer satisfaction survey template • Prepare consolidated score tracking template • Amend job descriptions and/or appoint a PMO lead for customer satisfaction reviews • Provide soft-skills training for those team members who need it	PMO, project managers, other team members who will be taking part in the Exceed reviews
6	Align service partners	• Introduce concept of customer satisfaction ratings and Exceed tool to service partners • Schedule satisfaction review meetings with service partners	PMO, project managers, relationship managers, service partners
7	Launch the Exceed process	• Schedule satisfaction review meeting with customers • Hold review meetings • Document outcomes	All parties including customers
8	Deliver on the issues	• Act on issues raised	Action owners

A FEW MONTHS INTO IMPLEMENTATION

Once the process is established and relationships built with the project manager, PMO and project team, simple techniques can be used to improve satisfaction ratings. Exceed is deliberately based upon simple concepts and subjective language. This is because perception is reality and perception is also subjective. If a project customer gave a project a score of, say, 5 (Acceptable) for communication, the project manager could say, 'You currently rate the project team as a 5 for communication. What do we have to do to be rated as 6, which is Good?' The customer will then provide the answer. If this action can be taken before returning the following month, the project manager can then collect the higher score at the next meeting.

Although the Exceed rating scale of 1 to 10 is simple, there are real differences between the numbers. A project manager can reasonably say, for example, 'You have rated us as Very Good, that's 8 out of 10, in terms of how we are managing your top project issues over the past three months. Shouldn't we now be calling that Consistently Very Good? We call that a 9.' This is not only fair and accurate but there is a specific reason for this approach. While Exceed is a simple methodology, easy to define and operate, it represents an extremely important and comprehensive commitment on the part of the project team. When the project team has delivered, it needs to be sure that the effort is recognized fairly. There is a significant difference between 'Very Good' and 'Consistently Very Good': namely, as we define it, consistent behaviour demonstrated over a three-month period.

As the customer-centric mindset takes hold and the Exceed meetings take place, the PMO may uncover project issues that will be difficult, impossible, unrealistic or uneconomic to resolve. They will no doubt also uncover particular project stakeholders who always assess the project teams more harshly than in other areas. All this is normal. Most customers are reasonable and will understand a well-presented argument when resolving a particular project issue is not considered possible or desirable. As the project managers get to grips with these challenges, the improved relationship and record of demonstrated successes will have an impact on collaborative project management techniques and increased levels of buy in from project customers.

BARRIERS TO CUSTOMER CENTRICITY

It would be great to think that project-based organizations and PMOs would jump at the opportunity to improve stakeholder engagement and project communication by using the Exceed process to demonstrate customer centricity. However, we acknowledge that there are likely to be some concerns about doing things differently, which will manifest themselves as barriers to a successful Exceed implementation. Below are some of the barriers, and a few recommendations for how they can be overcome.

Time

There have been times when more hard-headed and sceptical business leaders have stated that they have no time for a monthly Exceed meeting. This is not a problem. As we saw in Chapter 6, conference calls can be used successfully. Issues can be agreed, status discussed, priorities defined and scores obtained in a 15-minute phone call. You can even gather their feedback over email if necessary. Experience has shown that once successes have been delivered and the customer sees evidence that the process delivers real benefit to them, face-to-face meetings follow very quickly at the customer's request.

Transparency

Some leaders are averse to the idea of anything that sheds light on what could be seen as a poorly performing business unit. The Exceed process provides concrete scores that relate to how well the project manager and team are delivering, and by reflection, comment on the level of project management maturity in the organization. Fear that it is not as good as you had hoped can be a barrier to implementing this type of feedback loop. Honesty is essential for a successful PMO (Taylor 2011) and having access to this data across a number of projects will provide a way to run a health check on projects.

Remember, if you don't know how customers see their projects, project managers and their supporting PMO organization are not able to undertake course correction actions before the situation for the customer becomes untenable.

Transparency can also manifest itself in cultural issues. Team members or project customers from cultures that value harmony above transparency may find it difficult to share their honest thoughts during this process.

Team

Exceed is a process that can be seen as a way to rate individual project managers. If one project manager consistently receives excellent scores, and another does not, this is one way to distinguish between which project managers are well thought of in the organization and which are not. However, this can also be a dangerous approach to take, as project customers and their requirements vary significantly from project to project. A project manager who consistently receives average scores could be one of the top performers in the company, and as such is repeatedly assigned the more challenging projects and stakeholders. This will be reflected in the scores. 'People dislike measurements when they suspect that they will cast what they are doing in a bad light,' writes Kendrick (2012: 83), 'especially when there are potential adverse personal consequences.' Project managers will soon realize that scores can differ due to factors beyond their control and could be concerned that this will reflect badly on them. They may be resistant to the introduction of Exceed, even though they may support the concept of customer centricity.

A way to handle this is for the PMO to reassure project managers that Exceed scores will not be used to rank project managers. Of course, you then have to follow through on this – don't produce ranking of assessment data behind the scenes. Consideration should always be given to the context that the scores are received in. If this does not happen, the information provided will become unreliable as project managers seek to find ways around or out of carrying out satisfaction reviews. This is very much against the spirit of customer-centric project management.

If you are serious about creating a customer-centric project management environment, we recommend that you include the achievement of specific Exceed scores in project managers' objectives. However, to reduce resistance at an individual level, you could task a team of project managers with achieving an average Exceed score across a number of projects in a set time period, of, say, a year. In this way, there is an advantage for the project managers to work effectively together on the Exceed process, sharing the output from their discussions with their colleagues, and without the concern that one 'bad' project score will wipe out an individual's opportunity for a bonus.

Title

Customer satisfaction reviews are not just the project manager's role. The process is simple, and once you have the mindset of customer-centric project management and a couple of templates, it's easy enough for anyone to do. Don't limit Exceed to only those people with the job title of project manager, or any other individual title. Equally, don't let project team members use the fact that they do not have the title of project manager as reason to not adopt customer-centric project management principles or take an active part in customer satisfaction reviews.

Type of Organization

Thomas and Mullaly (2008) identified two types of project management culture. Project management was seen as either a tool for control or a leadership discipline. Organizations with a project management culture that leans towards adherence to process, structure and policing of control mechanisms are likely to struggle implementing Exceed, despite it being essentially another project management process. They will probably lack the flexibility to respond appropriately to the output of Exceed meetings and may be resistant to project managers having these discussions at all. Companies where project managers are seen as leaders and personal development is encouraged are likely to find lower barriers to resistance when implementing customer-centric project management techniques. A corporate culture that supports sharing of information and emphasizes coaching, mentoring and developing individuals is likely to consider Exceed as another opportunity to grow the capabilities of staff members.

Technique

In order to have meaningful conversations with project customers, project managers need to be equipped with the soft skills required to approach these conversations with confidence and emotional intelligence. The requirement for excellent soft skills is discussed in Chapter 9.

WHAT IF CUSTOMERS REFUSE TO ENGAGE?

There is always a risk that project customers will choose not to engage with the Exceed process, however you choose to implement it in your organization. Unwillingness to engage is still a type of engagement, in that it holds a mirror to the project and can help uncover underlying problems. Lack of engagement from stakeholders can also be an early warning sign that a project is in trouble (Williams 2007). Unwillingness to take part in an Exceed meeting could be a symptom of a project that management is hoping will go away or that is failing to meet its objectives in other areas. If all stakeholders are unwilling to engage with customer-centric project management approaches, this could be a sign that a project audit is in order. It would be worth assessing whether the project is still on target to deliver to its original business case. A decision about whether to continue with the project can be made after the review has taken place.

Sometimes lack of engagement hides the fact that closing down or cancelling projects is a difficult decision and perceived as a sign of failure. We would argue that closing down failing projects frees up resources to work on projects that will add value, so if your discussions with customers pick up on a lack of interest in projects, use this as an early warning sign to establish why this is the case and act accordingly.

KEY POINTS:

- Implementing Exceed in any organization is an eight-step process.
- Involve suppliers/partners in the process for the best chance of success. Project teams are their customers and in a collaborative environment they are also customers of project management processes.

- Using Exceed as a tool to deliver customer-centric project management may be met with resistance, but this can usually be overcome if it is adequately understood and if change management is used to gain buy in.
- Unwillingness to engage with the project team about satisfaction levels could be a sign of a project in distress.

CHAPTER 9

MOVING FORWARD WITH CUSTOMER-CENTRIC PROJECT MANAGEMENT

The ability to communicate at multiple levels is recognized as extremely important by managers (Starkweather and Stevenson 2011). Project managers need excellent interpersonal and soft skills in order to be able to have conversations about levels of satisfaction with project customers. These interpersonal skills and the ability to operate in a mature communicative way are often bundled under the heading of emotional intelligence. Clarke and Howell (2009) identified four project management competence areas associated to emotional intelligence: communication, teamwork, attentiveness and managing conflict. While an understanding of emotional intelligence across all competence areas is relevant for project managers in conversation with customers, the most relevant area is attentiveness.

MOVING FORWARD THROUGH ATTENTIVENESS

Clarke and Howell (2009) define attentiveness as including the ability to respond to and act upon concerns and issues, actively listening to other project team members and stakeholders and engaging stakeholders in the project. This is particularly relevant to Exceed as being attentive to stakeholders needs underpins the regular discussions about satisfaction. In addition, attentiveness includes the ability to follow through and act on the issues raised. Exceed as a process will fail if month after month stakeholders are raising the same issues because the project manager is not actively working to resolve them and has no update on what improvements are underway.

Before embarking on Exceed reviews with a project or number of projects it would be beneficial to assess the project manager's ability to be able to engage in this way. The following skills, knowledge and personal characteristics are key to successful stakeholder interaction:

- good listening skills;
- the ability to articulate issues in a non-judgemental way;

- the ability to facilitate discussion through probing questions;
- confidence;
- a belief in the concept of customer-centric project management and the importance of customer views;
- an understanding of the Exceed process and the rationale behind customer centricity;
- the ability to translate complex concepts into language the customer can understand without appearing condescending.

These skills are not that different to what is required for running projects, so the hope is that project managers will already be equipped to successfully deal with stakeholder conversations about satisfaction in an emotionally intelligent way. If not, consideration should be given about how to best equip the project management team to handle Exceed discussions.

MOVING FORWARD THROUGH EMPOWERING PROJECT MANAGERS

While project managers may have the skills, confidence and ability to handle Exceed conversations with project stakeholders, they need to feel empowered to do so. In a fluid operating environment where the internal political landscape can shift at short notice, project managers may feel reluctant to start building relationships with customers as it can expose them or their projects in ways that are not always flattering. Equally, managing a project over multiple locations may require travel in order to meet customers. Project managers should know that they are able to travel, to meet outsourcing partners or do anything else within reason deemed essential to ensure that Exceed reviews take place.

Knowing that they have their manager's, or the PMO's, support is especially important for project managers leading projects where the scores are likely to be perceived as 'bad'. If below-average scores are expected or received, line managers should not apportion blame or stigmatize the project manager in any way. Exceed provides a low-risk way to gather relevant qualitative data about the project and this can be used to constructively improve the way the project is run. Where scores are low, a more constructive managerial response is to provide support and encouragement combined with a pragmatic, achievable action plan towards providing a route to improved scores at the next meeting. Line managers, PMO coaches and mentors are well positioned to help project managers achieve this.

MOVING FORWARD THROUGH THE PMO

One way to ensure project managers genuinely feel empowered and that they have the support of the management team is to embed the concept of customer-centric project management in the form of Exceed practices into 'the way we do things here'. Standard templates and a consolidated, centralized method of recording aggregated results is one way to do this.

Another way is by including the gathering of Exceed scores and the resultant actions in the project managers' annual objectives and review progress during regular performance reviews. Managers can set targets for scores, either for an individual averaged across a year, a team averaged across a year or on a per project basis. We have seen a target of 6 (Good) for a team smashed in the first year of project managers being assessed in this way. In the subsequent year, the target was increased accordingly.

Another option is to amend the job description of the project manager, or any of the roles that will be carrying out Exceed reviews, to include a focus on customer-facing skills. This could mandate the amount of time a project manager is expected to spend working collaboratively with their customer. This will vary from project to project and perhaps from team member to team member. As we saw in Chapter 7 you may have appointed specific resources to carry out Exceed reviews and of course if that is the case these individuals will spend a higher proportion of their time with customers than other project managers.

MOVING FORWARD WITH CUSTOMER CENTRICITY

Building customer centricity into the way the PMO does business is our recommended approach, but you are free to take the principles we have shared in this book and adapt them as you see fit to ensure they work for your environment. As Winter et al. (2006) say, project management should be moving towards models that illuminate partial concepts and are not held up as the panacea for all complex projects. The world of project management, and projects themselves, is complicated and complex, and no one model can attempt to address every single element of the project management lifecycle. Instead, practitioners have to knit together models that make sense and add value in their own environments. As such, we have presented customer-centric project management as a mindset, and Exceed as a practical process, which can both go some way to helping project managers deliver a better service to their customer groups.

Many of the ideas we have presented in this book are not new, although they may be new to project management. It's not difficult to do customer-centric project management well, and as we have seen, Exceed is also a very simple process to use. It is like a contract between the project manager and the customer unit, in whatever shape is appropriate. The project manager will engage with them, listen to every issue, and resolve those issues rapidly. The project manager will continue the relationship regularly, provide a knowledgeable empowered interface with full backing and authority, operate against an agreed scoring mechanism, be honest in situations where resolution is not possible or economic and will explain why. Also, and most importantly, they will maintain a firm and steady resolve way beyond the time when the customer unit first returns scores of Good, Very Good or Excellent.

The central pillar of customer centricity – the key takeaway from this whole book – is that customers count. Continual and specific engagement for the good of all customers involved in delivery of projects – those who deliver, those who underpin project delivery teams and those for whom delivery is provided – is the way that we will improve project success rates. When customer-centric project management becomes 'the way we do things here' then project managers will know how all of their customers are feeling all of the time and what their top issues are and can, therefore, always refer to actions which reflect what needs to be done to provide a good experience all along the way.

This moves the emphasis to the customer experience over time and away from the post-mortem or post-implementation review. Customer-centric project management seeks to equip the project manager with full knowledge of the vital signs and feelings of every project stakeholders on such a regular basis that PIR or post-mortem situations become less important.

In project management terms, we find the use of some industry accepted language interesting. It is impossible to disassociate the term 'post-mortem' from unhappy events. Post-mortems are required not only when someone has died (not the most uplifting image), but when the death was unexpected or suspicious. Moreover, reasons have to be found and made public. 'Post-mortem' suggests bad news. To our knowledge no one has ever carried out a post-mortem on someone who died laughing. Projects, and project managers, don't need the baggage associated with this term, and we would suggest that if the project is going to be subjected to this level of forensic scrutiny then the project team have missed an opportunity to audit, review, improve and potentially close the project down before it got to the end.

Here's one final example. Think of project management in terms of flying a plane. The pilot (the project manager) needs dials and levers. Dials let him know what is going on in his engines, fuel tanks, oil reserves, his position against course and bearing, and the status of the landing gear. The levers let him take action to fly the plane smoothly by making adjustments to trim, elevation, direction and speed. Customer-centric project management provides the mechanism for project managers to have their own set of dials and levers. The Exceed process provides the dials; the customer-centric mindset provides the levers. However, we go one step further than that: customer centricity includes indicators from the perception of passengers and crew, not just at the end of the flight but from runway to runway.

This complete view of ongoing satisfaction is highly valuable in framing an overall picture of the health and complete status of the project, project management team or portfolio. When a PMO is working in a customer-centric way, the project managers can operate with a high level of confidence that each customer group is relatively content and that the delivery teams are performing to plan. Knowing this is the case breeds confidence and a positive mindset, which in turn contributes to project success levels, as Lechler and Byrne (2010) conclude.

On the other hand, poor performance within a narrow set of measures not aimed at customers can breed disquiet amongst stakeholder groups. Using our aeroplane analogy, a highly nervous airline passenger who flips down the tray at his seat and finds it stained with coffee rings is likely to wonder what else hasn't been serviced properly.

Project managers want to work with engaged, supportive customers who are involved, but not nervous, every step of the way. Collaborating with customers can improve project success rates, however you choose to define success. Customer-centric project management helps project managers take collaboration to the next level, and provides the opportunity to bring project managers closer to understanding the project experience of their customers at any point in the lifecycle. The Exceed process elicits, records, measures and monitors customer satisfaction rates and by following the process fully there is an excellent chance companies will see their projects and project teams rated as Good, Very Good or Excellent.

Who wouldn't want that?

KEY POINTS:

- Customer-centric project management requires project managers to have excellent interpersonal skills.
- Once the customer-centric mindset is embedded, build Exceed into the framework of the PMO using standard templates.
- Set realistic targets and don't use the metrics to apportion blame.
- Engage and listen to your project customers, act on their concerns and see the impact on project success.

CARRY ON THE DISCUSSION

We want your project to be better and we'd like to hear about ways in which you are implementing customer-centric project management in your organization. You can find us online at www.customercentricpm.com. Please stop by and say hello.

SHARE THESE IDEAS

We think customer-centric project management and Exceed are great things and, if you do too, you can help spread the word about these concepts. Please consider doing something to help the ideas reach a wider audience. Here are some suggestions:

- Write a review of this book on Amazon or your favourite online bookstore.
- Mention customer-centric project management or this book on Twitter, LinkedIn, your blog or your favourite social media site.
- Leave this book prominently on your desk for your colleagues in your PMO to flick through.
- Talk about the ideas in this book at a 'lunch and learn' session, and share the concepts with your colleagues.
- Be more customer-centric!

Thank you for your support.

APPENDIX 1: EXCEED ISSUES LIST FROM SPIRE HEALTHCARE'S INITIAL IMPLEMENTATION

Site	Type	Description
Hospital 1	Top 3 issue	Unable to use PC in Ward 1 since migration
	Top 3 issue	Still waiting on two PCs for theatres
	Top 3 issue	Users unable get Pathology results from new printer
	Communication	Service Centre does not keep customer updated with progress
	Proactivity	Not very proactive; customer having to chase for updates
	Service quality	Customer experiencing problems getting through to Service Centre. Hardware is not being repaired as fast as expected
Hospital 2	Top 3 issue	System X licence required
	Top 3 issue	Service Centre delay in answering phone
	Top 3 issue	Data encryption for sending booking forms via email is required
	Communication	Channels of communication are not clear
	Proactivity	IT is never proactive, the customer always has to chase
	Service quality	Service Centre is not answering the phone quickly enough. However, they are very good
Hospital 3	Top 3 issue	Getting through to the Service Centre
	Top 3 issue	Duplicate IP address causing problems
	Top 3 issue	Generic password problem
	Communication	Unhappy with the lack of communication from the Service Centre. Customer constantly having to chase
	Proactivity	Not very proactive; customer having chase

	Service quality	Quality is a bit of a mix; some good experiences and some bad
Hospital 4	Top 3 issue	Response times when ordering hardware. Customer is still waiting for a consultant's PC to be delivered
	Top 3 issue	A printer was ordered 3 months ago and the customer is still waiting
	Top 3 issue	They delay in getting new user accounts created
	Communication	The migration communication was good and customers has been kept informed with current status
	Proactivity	Satisfied with current service level
	Service quality	Service Centre has been very professional and as promised they always revert back
Hospital 5	Top 3 issue	Consultant access to IT in general, i.e. wifi
	Top 3 issue	Access to Service Centre
	Top 3 issue	Consultants being able to access their clinic list remotely or locally
	Communication	Communication has improved. Sometimes there is over communication but timeliness is better
	Proactivity	We are more proactive
	Service quality	An improvement from what we previously had
Hospital 6	Top 3 issue	Still waiting to add a new consultant onto System X
	Top 3 issue	Remote access for Ops Manager is required
	Top 3 issue	Length of time on hold trying to get through to Service Centre
	Communication	Communication relating to migrations was very good, however some communications are too technical
	Proactivity	The Customer Service Manager being on board is really good and can see improvements. However, having to always chase the Service Centre for updates
	Service quality	This we scored as consistently poor due to the level of service received from the Service Centre, the length of time people are on hold and having to chase for updates

APPENDIX 2: GENERIC PROJECT EXCEED SURVEY TEMPLATE

Exceed Customer Satisfaction Record				

Project Manager Name		Respondent Name		

Date of Meeting:	Date	Period Covered:	Month	Score
Managing current issues				5
Do we fix things in a timely manner?		Verbatim comments in here		5
Are we responsive to project issues?				5
Communication				8
How good are the project communications?		Verbatim comments in here		8
Integration				9
How well is the new software integrated?		Verbatim comments in here		8
How have the training, support and documentation been so far?				10
How is it going overall?				7
What's your general level of satisfaction with this project at the moment?		Verbatim comments in here		7
			Average Score	
			Service	7.25

APPENDIX 3: TAILORED PROJECT EXCEED SURVEY TEMPLATE

Exceed Customer Satisfaction Record				

Programme Manager Name	**Stakeholder/Customer Group** Name

Date of Meeting:	**Date**	**Period Covered:**	**Month**	**Score**
Top three issues				5
1	Current issue 1	Verbatim comments in here		3
2	Current issue 2			5
3	Current issue 3			7
Communication				6.5
Quality of written and verbal communications from project team		Verbatim comments in here		6
Clarity of plans and scope of stakeholder involvement				7
Quality and regularity of status information				´ 7
Proactivity				8
Clear statement of activities and priorities		Verbatim comments in here		8
Timeliness of stakeholder involvement				8
Communication of changes				8
Quality of project delivery				8
Perceived level of engagement		Verbatim comments in here		6
Confidence in success of project aims (how is it going?)				10

	Average Score
Service	6.8

APPENDIX 4: SAMPLE JOB DESCRIPTION TEXT

OVERVIEW

In conjunction with the head of PMO, take ownership of the customer relationship for the project management services delivered to [your company or client]. Develop strong business relationships, which involve spending at least [x] per cent of available time in contact with key project customers.

KEY OBJECTIVES AND ACCOUNTABILITIES

- Act as prime customer interface for customer care.
- Develop business relationships with a cross-section of the project customer base in order to improve the services provided and raise the profile of the project management function in [your company].
- Identify and understand all customer requirements.
- Own every customer-related service issue.
- Bring service issues raised by the customer to a conclusion that meets the customer requirements.
- Agree specific Exceed measures with each project customer in support of the Exceed process.
- Agree the frequency of Exceed discussions with the customer. These to be at least monthly.
- Agree ongoing Exceed satisfaction ratings with the project customer on a regular basis.
- Work with other supporting business areas and service partners to identify and resolve service issues and improve services provided.
- Act as prime internal interface to gain full understanding of proposed strategic and tactical change and the potential effect on the customer.
- Identify service improvement options.
- Identify multiple-user contact strategies and methods which reflect business importance and the benefits derived.

KEY ATTITUDES AND BEHAVIOURS

- Deal with customers and colleagues with courtesy, professionalism and integrity.
- Ensure the project customer has a full understanding as to why decisions are made.
- Identify, recommend and communicate improvements to PMO processes and procedures.
- Consistently adhere to standards and processes.
- Focus toward colleagues and their requirements.
- Actively promote team spirit and mutual support.
- Contribute positively at all times.
- Do not promise what you cannot deliver.
- Always deliver what you promise.

REFERENCES

Andersen, E. 2010. 'Are We Getting Any Better? Comparing Project Management in the Years 2000 and 2008'. *Project Management Journal* 41(4), 4–16.

Atkinson, R. 1999. 'Project Management: Cost, Time and Quality, Two Best Guesses and a Phenomenon, It's Time to Accept Other Success Criteria'. *International Journal of Project Management* 17(6), 337–42.

Aubry, M. and Hobbs, B. 2011. 'A Fresh Look at the Contribution of Project Management to Organizational Performance'. *Project Management Journal* 42(1), 3–16.

Barefoot, D. and Szabo, J. 2010. *Friends with Benefits: A Social Media Marketing Handbook*. San Fransisco: No Starch Press.

Bicknell, D. 2009. 'Collaboration Drives Innovation'. *Computer Weekly* 28(April), 14–16.

Bowles, M. 2011. Keeping Score. *PM Network*, May 2011, 50–54.

Chiocchio, F., Forgues, D., Paradis, D. et al. 2011. 'Teamwork in Integrated Design Projects: Understanding the Effects of Trust, Conflict, and Collaboration on Performance'. *Project Management Journal* 42(6), 78–91.

Clarke, N. and Howell, R. 2009. *Emotional Intelligence and Projects*. Newtown Square: PMI.

Collyer, S., Warren, C., Hemsley, B. et al. 2010. 'Aim, Fire, Aim: Project Planning Styles in Dynamic Environments'. *Project Management Journal* 41(4), 108–21.

Dietrich, P., Eskerod, P., Dalcher, D. et al. 2010. 'The Dynamics of Collaboration in Multipartner Projects'. *Project Management Journal* 41(4), 59–78.

Dvir, D., Lipovetsky, S., Shenhar, A. et al. 1998. 'In Search of Project Classification: A Non-Universal Approach to Project Success Factors'. *Research Policy* 27, 915–35.

Fader, P. 2011. *Customer Centricity*. Philadelphia: Wharton Digital Press.

Finklestein, J. 2012. *Fuse*. Austin: Greenleaf Book Group Press.

Future Changes/TCW. 2009. Why Businesses Don't Collaborate. [Online]. Available at: http://www.scribd.com/doc/16336782/Why-Businesses-Dont-Collaborate-Meeting-Management-Group-Input-and-Wiki-Usage-Survey-Results [accessed: 23 January 2012].

Geoghegan, L. and Dulewicz, V. 2008. 'Do Project Managers' Leadership Competencies contribute to Project Success?' *Project Management Journal* 39(4), 58–67.

Harrin, E. 2010. *Social Media for Project Managers*. Newtown Square: PMI.

Herzog, V.L. 2001. 'Trust Building on Corporate Collaborative Project Teams'. *Project Management Journal* 32(1), 28–37.

Hyväri, I. 2006. 'Success of Projects in Different Organizational Conditions'. *Project Management Journal* 37(4), 31–41.

Jaafari, A. 2003. 'Project Management in the Age of Complexity and Change'. *Project Management Journal* 34(4), 47–57.

Jaffe, J. 2007. *Join the Conversation*. Hoboken: Wiley.

Johnson, M. and Johnson, L. 2010. *Generations, Inc: From Boomers to Linksters: Managing the Friction between Generations at Work*. New York: Amacom.

Juli, T. 2011. *Leadership Principles for Project Success*. Boca Raton: CRC Press.

Kendrick, T. 2012. *Results Without Authority*. 2nd edn. New York: Amacom.

Kerzner, H. and Saladis, F. 2009. *Value Driven Project Management*. New York: Wiley.

Khang, D.B. and Moe, T.L. 2008. 'Success Criteria and Factors for International Development Projects: A Life-Cycle-Based Framework'. *Project Management Journal* 39(3), 72–84.

Klakegg, O.J., Williams, T., Walker, D., Andersen, B. and Magnussen, O.M. 2010. *Early Warning Signs in Complex Projects*. Newtown Square: PMI.

KPMG. 2005. Global IT Project Management Survey. [Online]. Available at: http://www.kpmg.com/CN/en/IssuesAndInsights/ArticlesPublications/Documents/Global-IT-Project-Management-Survey-0508.pdf [accessed: 23 January 2012].

Lechler, T.G. and Byrne, J.C. 2010. *The Mindset for Creating Project Value*. Newtown Square: PMI.

Littau, P., Jujagiri, N.J. and Adlbrecht, G. 2010. '25 Years of Stakeholder Theory in Project Management Literature (1984–2009)'. *Project Management Journal* 41(4), 17–29.

Madsen, S. 2011. *The Project Management Coaching Workbook: Six Steps to Unleashing Your Potential*. Vienna: Management Concepts.

Moore, S. 2010. *Strategic Project Portfolio Management*. Hoboken: Wiley.

OGC. 2009. *Managing Successful Projects with PRINCE2*. London: TSO.

Papke-Shields, K.E., Beise, C. and Quan, J. 2010. 'Do Project Managers Practice What they Preach, and Does It Matter to Project Success?' *International Journal of Project Management* 28(7), 650–62.

Pennypacker, J. 2009. Project Portfolio Management circa 2025, in *Project Management Circa 2025*, edited by D.I. Cleland and B. Bidanda. Newtown Square: PMI, 215–26.

Preble, J.F. 2005. 'Toward a Comprehensive Model of Stakeholder Engagement'. *Business and Society Review* 110(4), 407–31.

Project Management Institute. 2008. *A Guide to the Project Management Body of Knowledge*. 4th edn. Newtown Square: PMI.

Sauer, C. and Reich, B.H. 2009. 'Rethinking IT Project Management: Evidence of a New Mindset and Its Implications'. *International Journal of Project Management* 27, 182–93.

Sewchurran, K. and Barron, M. 2008. 'An Investigation into Successfully Managing and Sustaining the Project Sponsor–Project Manager Relationship Using Soft Systems Methodology'. *Project Management Journal* 39(Supplement), 56–68.

Shenhar, A.J. and Dvir, D. 2007. *Reinventing Project Management*. Boston: Harvard Business School Press.

Shenhar, A.J., Tishler, A., Dvir, D. et al. 2002. 'Refining the Search for Project Success Factors: A Multivariate, Typological Approach'. *R & D Management* 32(2), 111–26.

Starkweather, J.A. and Stevenson, D.H. 2011. 'PMP® Certification as a Core Competency: Necessary but Not Sufficient'. *Project Management Journal* 42(1), 31–41.

Suhonen, M. and Paasivaara, L. 2011. 'Shared Human Capital in Project Managment: A Systematic Review of the Literature'. *Project Management Journal* 42(2), 4–16.

Tabaka, J. 2006. *Collaboration Explained: Facilitation Skills for Software Project Leaders*. Upper Saddle River: Pearson Education Inc.

Taylor, P. 2011. *Leading Successful PMOs*. Farnham: Gower.

Thomas, J. and Mullaly, M. 2008. *Researching the Value of Project Management*. Newtown Square: PMI.

Wake, S. 2008. *EVA in the UK*. 8th edn. London: Steve Wake Projects Ltd.

Weinstein, J. and Jaques, T. 2009. State Government: Project Management 2025, in *Project Management circa 2025*, edited by D.I. Cleland and B. Bidanda. Newtown Square: PMI, 345–61.

White, D. and Fortune, J. 2002. 'Current Practice in Project Management: An Empirical Study'. *International Journal of Project Management* 20, 1–11.

Williams, P. 2007. 'Make Sure You Get a Positive Return'. *ComputerWeekly* 13(November), 18–20.

Winter, M., Smith, C., Morris, P. et al. 2006. 'Directions for Future Research in Project Management: The Main Findings of a UK Government-Funded Research Network'. *International Journal of Project Management* 24, 638–49.

Zhai, L., Xin, Y. and Cheng, C. 2009. 'Understanding the Value of Project Management from a Stakeholder's Perspective: Case Study of Mega-Project Management'. *Project Management Journal* 40(1), 99–109.

LICENSING

We want your projects to be better. You are free to use and adapt the ideas in this book and to implement Exceed and the principles of customer-centric project management in your organization. However, the 8-step Exceed implementation plan, the Exceed name and the Exceed templates provided in this book are the copyright of Phil Peplow. That means you cannot sell them, so please don't. Thank you.

INDEX

ADVANCES IN PROJECT MANAGEMENT

Advances in Project Management provides short, state of play guides to the main aspects of the new emerging applications, including: maturity models, agile projects, extreme projects, Six Sigma and projects, human factors and leadership in projects, project governance, value management, virtual teams and project benefits.

CURRENTLY PUBLISHED TITLES

Managing Project Uncertainty, David Cleden 978-0-566-08840-7

Strategic Project Risk Appraisal and Management, Elaine Harris 978-0-566-08848-3

Project-Oriented Leadership, Ralf Müller and J. Rodney Turner 978-0-566-08923-7

Tame, Messy and Wicked Risk Leadership, David Hancock 978-0-566-09242-8

Managing Project Supply Chains, Ron Basu 978-1-4094-2515-1

Second Order Project Management, Michael Cavanagh 978-1-4094-1094-2

Sustainability in Project Management, Gilbert Silvius, Ron Schipper, Julia Planko, Jasper van den Brink and Adri Köhler 978-1-4094-3169-5

The Spirit of Project Management, Judi Neal and Alan Harpham 978-1-4094-0959-5

REVIEWS OF THE SERIES

Managing Project Uncertainty, David Cleden

> *This is a must-read book for anyone involved in project management. The author's carefully crafted work meets all my "4Cs" review criteria. The book is clear, cogent, concise and complete ... it is a brave author who essays to write about managing project uncertainty in a text extending to only 117 pages (soft-cover version). In my opinion, David Cleden succeeds brilliantly. ... For project managers this book, far from being a short-lived stress anodyne, will provide a confidence-boosting tonic. Project uncertainty? Bring it on, I say!*
>
> International Journal of Managing Projects in Business

> *Uncertainty is an inevitable aspect of most projects, but even the most proficient project manager struggles to successfully contain it. Many projects overrun and consume more funds than were originally budgeted, often leading to unplanned expense and outright programme failure. David examines how uncertainty occurs and provides management strategies that the user can put to immediate use on their own project work. He also provides a series of pre-emptive uncertainty and risk avoidance strategies that should be the cornerstone of any planning exercise for all personnel involved in project work.*
>
> *I have been delivering both large and small projects and programmes in the public and private sector since 1989. I wish this book had been available when I began my career in project work. I strongly commend this book to all project professionals.*
>
> Lee Hendricks, Sales & Marketing Director,
> SunGard Public Sector

> *The book under review is an excellent presentation of a comprehensive set of explorations about uncertainty (its recognition) in the context of projects. It does a good job of all along reinforcing the difference between risk (known unknowns) management and managing uncertainty (unknown unknowns – "bolt from the blue"). The author lucidly presents a variety of frameworks/ models so that the reader easily grasps the varied forms in which uncertainty presents itself in the context of projects.*
>
> VISION: The Journal of Business Perspective (India)

> *Cleden will leave you with a sound understanding about the traits, tendencies, timing and tenacity of uncertainty in projects. He is also adept at identifying certain methods that try to contain the uncertainty, and why some prove more successful than others. Those who expect risk management to be the be-all, end-all for uncertainty solutions will be in for a rude awakening.*
>
> Brad Egeland, Project Management Tips

Strategic Project Risk Appraisal and Management, Elaine Harris

> *Elaine Harris's volume is timely. In a world of books by "instant experts" it's pleasing to read something by someone who clearly knows their onions, and has a passion for the subject. In summary, this is a thorough and engaging book.*
>
> > Chris Morgan, Head of Business Assurance for Select Plant Hire,
> > Quality World

> *As soon as I met Elaine I realised that we both shared a passion to better understand the inherent risk in any project, be that capital investment, expansion capital or expansion of assets. What is seldom analysed are the components of knowledge necessary to make a good judgement, the impact of our own prejudices in relation to projects or for that matter the cultural elements within an organisation which impact upon the decision making process. Elaine created a system to break this down and give reasons and logic to both the process and the human interaction necessary to improve the chances of success. Adopting her recommendations will improve teamwork and outcomes for your company.*
>
> > Edward Roderick Hon. LLD, former CEO Christian Salvesen plc

Project-Oriented Leadership, Ralf Müller and J Rodney Turner

> *Müller and Turner have compiled a terrific "ready-reckoner" that all project managers would benefit from reading and reflecting upon to challenge their performance. The authors have condensed considerable experience and research from a wide variety of professional disciplines, to provide a robust digest that highlights the significance of leadership capabilities for effective delivery of project outcomes. One of the big advantages of this book is the richness of the content and the natural flow of their argument throughout such a short book....Good advice, well explained and backed up with a body of evidence...I will be recommending the book to colleagues who are in project leader and manager roles and to students who are considering these as part of their development or career path.'*
>
> > Arthur Shelley, RMIT University, Melbourne, Australia, International
> > Journal of Managing Projects in Business

> *In a remarkably succinct 89 pages, Müller and Turner review an astonishing depth of evidence, supported by their own (published) research which challenges many of the commonly held assumptions not only about project management, but about what makes for successful leaders.*
>
> *This book is clearly written more for the project-manager type personality than for the natural leader. Concision, evidence and analysis are the main characteristics of the writing style...it is massively authoritative, and so*

carefully written that a couple of hours spent in its 89 pages may pay huge dividends compared to the more expansive, easy reading style of other management books.

Mike Turner, Director of Communications for NHS Warwickshire

Tame, Messy and Wicked Risk Leadership, David Hancock

This book takes project risk management firmly onto a higher and wider plane. We thought we knew what project risk management was and what it could do. David Hancock shows us a great deal more of both. David Hancock has probably read more about risk management than almost anybody else; he has almost certainly thought about it as much as anybody else and he has quite certainly learnt from doing it on very difficult projects as much as anybody else. His book draws fully on all three components. For a book which tackles a complex subject with breadth, insight and novelty – it's remarkable that it is also a really good read. I could go on!

Dr Martin Barnes CBE FREng, President,
The Association for Project Management

This compact and thought-provoking description of risk management will be useful to anybody with responsibilities for projects, programmes or businesses. It hits the nail on the head in so many ways, for example by pointing out that risk management can easily drift into a checklist mindset, driven by the production of registers of numerous occurrences characterised by the Risk = Probablity × Consequence equation. David Hancock points out that real life is much more complicated, with the heart of the problem lying in people, so that real life resembles poker rather than roulette. He also points out that while the important thing is to solve the right problem, many real-life issues cannot be readily described in a definitive statement of the problem. There are often interrelated individual problems with surrounding social issues and he describes these real-life situations as "Wicked Messes". Unusual terminology, but definitely worth the read, as much for the overall problem description as for the recommended strategies for getting to grips with real-life risk management. I have no hesitation in recommending this book.

Sir Robert Walmsley KCB FREng, Chairman of the Board of the Major
Projects Association

In highlighting the complexity of many of today's problems and defining them as tame, messy or wicked, David Hancock brings a new perspective to the risk issues that we currently face. He challenges risk managers, and particularly those involved in project risk management, to take a much broader approach to the assessment of risk and consider the social, political and behavioural dimensions of each problem, as well as the scientific and engineering aspects with which they are most comfortable.

In this way, risks will be viewed more holistically and managed more effectively than at present.

Dr Lynn T. Drennan, Chief Executive Alarm,
The Public Risk Management Association

ABOUT THE EDITOR

Professor Darren Dalcher is founder and Director of the National Centre for Project Management, a Professor of Software Project Management at Middlesex University and Visiting Professor of Computer Science at the University of Iceland. Professor Dalcher has been named by the Association for Project Management as one of the top 10 'movers and shapers' in project management. He has also been voted *Project Magazine*'s Academic of the Year for his contribution in 'integrating and weaving academic work with practice'.

Professor Dalcher is active in numerous international committees, steering groups and editorial boards. He is heavily involved in organising international conferences, and has delivered many keynote addresses and tutorials. He has written over 150 papers and book chapters on project management and software engineering. He is Editor-in-Chief of *Software Process Improvement and Practice*, an international journal focusing on capability, maturity, growth and improvement.

Professor Dalcher is a Fellow of the Association for Project Management and the British Computer Society, and a Member of the Project Management Institute, the Academy of Management, the Institute for Electrical and Electronics Engineers and the Association for Computing Machinery. He is a Chartered IT Practitioner. He is a member of the PMI Advisory Board responsible for the prestigious David I. Cleland project management award, and of the APM Professional Development Board.

National Centre for Project Management
Middlesex University
College House
Trent Park
Bramley Road
London N14 4YZ
Email: ncpm@mdx.ac.uk
Phone: +44 (0)20 8411 2299

40779603R00078

Printed in Poland
by Amazon Fulfillment
Poland Sp. z o.o., Wrocław